Women's Troubles

Manchester University Press

Women's Troubles

Gender and feminist politics in post-Agreement Northern Ireland

Claire Pierson

MANCHESTER UNIVERSITY PRESS

Copyright © Claire Pierson 2025

The right of Claire Pierson to be identified as the author of this work has been asserted in accordance with the Copyright, Designs and Patents Act 1988.

Published by Manchester University Press
Oxford Road, Manchester, M13 9PL

www.manchesteruniversitypress.co.uk

British Library Cataloguing-in-Publication Data
A catalogue record for this book is available from the British Library

ISBN   978 1 5261 6180 2   hardback

First published 2025

The publisher has no responsibility for the persistence or accuracy of URLs for any external or third-party internet websites referred to in this book, and does not guarantee that any content on such websites is, or will remain, accurate or appropriate.

EU authorised representative for GPSR:
Easy Access System Europe, Mustamäe tee 50, 10621 Tallinn, Estonia
gpsr.requests@easproject.com

Typeset
by Deanta Global Publishing Services, Chennai, India

Contents

Acknowledgements	*page* vi
Introduction	1
1 Gender identities and political spaces	17
2 Feminist movement building and collective identity	38
3 Gender experts, participation and policy making	62
4 Women, peace and security? Gender-based violence, legacies of conflict and masculinities	85
5 Beyond the state: prefigurative politics and abortion care activism	105
Conclusion	126
References	135
Index	154

Acknowledgements

First, it is important to acknowledge that this book could not exist without the participation of all those who spoke to me for this project and previous research. Their words have shaped my thinking and the direction of this project.

Thanks are due to many friends and colleagues who read drafts of chapters and provided thoughtful and helpful commentary including Gemma Bird, Fiona Bloomer, Maria Deiana, Sarah Jankowitz and Noirin MacNamara. I have presented parts of this book at various conferences and workshops including the Political Studies Association of Ireland annual conference, the 'Imagining Common Grounds' conference at the University of Duisburg, the 'Abortion in Ireland: Access, Experience, and Provision' workshop at the University of Lincoln and the 'Doing Public Engagement on Violence' workshop at the University of Liverpool. Conversations and feedback from these discussions have proven invaluable in thinking through many parts of the book. All errors are of course my own.

Finally, the cover image from this book was provided by artist, academic and activist Emma Campbell (a member of the 2021 Turner Prize winning Array Collective). Entitled 'Regalia: The Slapper', the sculpture made from Lego and Lego-style blocks subverts patriarchal power, into justice and self-determination through compassion. Inspired by Bernadette Devlin McAliskey, who famously slapped the British Home Secretary after he lied about Bloody Sunday, who continues her social justice work today across the island of Ireland, including abortion rights, LGBTQIA+, migrant and refugee rights as well as solidarity across race and class. Regalia: The Slapper, is inspired by the rubber gloves of domestic labour, and hidden reproductive work, also attested to by the use of children's toy bricks.

Introduction

'Theories of transformation, and transformation itself, suggest a movement, a shifting of things from 'here' to 'there' – whether 'there' is imagined to be 'before' or 'beyond' or to inhere in certain elements 'within' the present. It involves a movement from a form or place we might recognize to something or somewhere else – or in some pessimistic accounts, quite simply straight back 'here' again, as if there had been no change at all.' (Robinson, 2000: 286).

Feminism's core goal is to transform gendered power relations whether that is in localised social and political spaces or in global, transnational movements. How this goal is to be achieved, and exactly what a feminist future will look like, is contested. For some it will be achieved through liberal equality in the form of institutional representation and legislative and policy change to lessen material inequalities, whilst for others more radical measures will be needed such as reimagining, fundamentally challenging, and perhaps eradicating, both institutions and the socially determined categories of gender.

Rich descriptions and analyses of processes and challenges of feminist transformation help us to imagine potential social and political futures. Whilst there are contextual specificities and strategies developed in particular circumstances, there are often glimpses of possibility which can invigorate and guide those working in other locations. Feminist interventions in political spaces and waves of feminist activism and thought are often considered through the examples of long-standing, peaceful liberal democracies, yet there is value in analysis emerging from regions which have undergone significant political and institutional shifts. As Tripp (2023: 922) writes:

> while there are multiple paths to expanding women's citizenship, the opportunities that emerge with 'critical junctures', such as the end of conflict and revolution, show that the expansion of women's political rights can be accelerated as a by-product of such social rupture, especially when combined with pressure from women's movements and activists. These 'critical junctures' are

short periods of time which increase the probability that actors can intervene to bring about long-term institutional transformation.

Northern Ireland's (NI) feminist movement could be described within the feminist wave metaphor as a movement 'lost between the waves' (see Graff, 2003, who uses this phrasing to describe the Polish context). This idea of being lost comes from a sense of not fitting into the chronological framing of feminist movements which presents an (arguably false) linearity to the development of ideas and the achievement of equality. There is value in investigating feminism in spaces which have been seen to get 'lost between the waves'. These societies have had to navigate complexity and difference, and maintain movements in very challenging circumstances and, rather than being seen as outliers, have valuable lessons for other contexts.

This sense of being 'lost' also relates to geographical location and constitutional status. Being between British and Irish feminisms, yet with a distinct movement of its own, often means being peripheral and unintelligible to both. With the region coming into global focus most recently for its restrictive abortion laws (repealed in 2019), it could be assumed that there is less coordinated feminist organising than in other global north contexts. However, this assumption would be false. There is a strong coalition of women's community groups and organisations, feminist activists and academics who create a networked tapestry working towards a diverse range of feminist goals. Many of the issues and challenges presented throughout this book will be recognisable to those familiar with contemporary feminist organising, yet there are distinct strategies and discourses emerging contextually in NI influenced both by global movements and by histories of organising in the shadow of violent conflict and sectarianism.

This is where this book intervenes. I take seriously Tripps' (2023) claim about critical junctures and how changes in social and political climate can shape the emergence of movements, their goals and strategies and potentially challenge traditional gender orders. Taking the Northern Ireland (NI) peace agreement (the Good Friday or Belfast Agreement, hereafter, the Agreement) as a critical juncture point, this book will provide a close examination of feminist activity in a variety of political spheres, addressing both the challenges that continue to impede feminist transformations and the interventions which have furthered gender equality and reshaped political spaces. This text, however, takes a longer lens, examining feminist movement building approximately twenty-five years after the Agreement, arguing that this critical juncture enabled alternative political identities to emerge and begin to create and shape political landscapes.

The Agreement represents an important juncture, where society and its political institutions were being redefined and reconstituted, equality (in theory) was being written into legislation and practice and, at the same time, widespread initiatives were developed to redefine social relations, albeit within and between the traditional two communities. Whilst this book is not primarily interested in 'post-conflict' relations, this period of social and political restructuring presents a starting point for political analysis of alternative political identities. In addition to this, the recent global rise in feminist activism, conceptualised as the fourth wave, can also be seen in the NI context (Deiana, 2013; Pierson, 2018b; Deiana and Pierson, 2015). As Deiana and Pierson (2015) write, 'the picture emerging from Northern Ireland is one of a concerted effort to radically improve the position of women and re-shape society through the principle of gender equality' where 'continuities and ruptures among different generations are nothing but a strength which equips feminism(s) with the ability to develop, adapt and respond to the evolving challenges that sexism, patriarchy, and exclusions around the axis of class, ethnicity, sexuality and ability present at specific times.' This presents an opportune moment to examine the strategies, discourses and processes adopted by feminist actors, the challenges they have encountered and the transformations that feminist activity has been able to make.

This book therefore sits at the intersection between the global literature on contemporary feminist organising and feminist analysis of transitions from violent conflict. Specifically, I will address the relationship between advances in feminist movement building and activism and the transition from violent conflict in Northern Ireland, asking how political space has been shaped and changed in this context by feminist and gender actors and to what extent this has enabled transformations in gender relations and equality. I do not see political activity as solely operating through formal political institutions and, whilst I do consider this (in Chapter 3), more space is given to thinking through alternative political spaces and different ways of acting politically, such as feminist care giving practices (Chapter 5).

Contemporary feminism, transforming gender relations and political spaces

Contemporary feminist movements work within a particularly interesting global political moment. A noticeable renewal of interest in feminism and in feminist organising since 2010 has been termed fourth wave feminism (Munro, 2013). As discussed in Chapter 2 in more depth, the fourth wave, whilst contested, encompasses a commitment to intersectionality, to the recognition of privilege and attempts to renegotiate power in feminist groups through ceding space to marginalised groups. The fourth wave has largely been exemplified through the rise in online spaces and their use in activism and organising. The majority of the literature concerning this new wave of British feminism has not considered Northern Ireland. When Northern Ireland is written about, it is often because of the ban on abortion or the status of same-sex marriage, both legalised in 2019. This has the effect of positioning NI as behind or, as mentioned earlier, 'lost between the waves'. This positioning neglects the diversity of organising and the fact that, historically, attention to equality and rights during the period of conflict (which also loosely overlapped with the second-wave feminist movement) was on civil rights, ending political violence and challenging sectarianism and NI's feminist movement focused its energies on building support systems in communities (see the following chapter for a more detailed discussion of feminist organising in the north of Ireland).

It is important to be clear that this book does not assume a feminist movement emerged solely from the post-conflict period onwards. There is a legacy of feminist activism and a definitive overlap in feminist actors, whilst often the same issues are being argued for, there is a sharing of learning and new strategies being undertaken. Cynthia Cockburn described this new feminism in her 'retrospective' of Belfast feminism as post-millennial feminism, 'rather than being embedded in the working-class struggle in housing estates and workplaces, is a movement mainly of educated women, students, confident in their social networking skills. It has its own priorities—sexuality, reproductive rights, multiculturalism and violence against women—in contrast to the policy-challenging agenda of socialism, inclusion and workers' rights inspired by the former alliance of community centres and trade unions' (Cockburn, 2013: 10). Whilst there are new strategies of feminism emerging, I argue that this is still embedded within a recognition of, and fight against, material inequality (see Pierson, 2018b).

Internationally, increasing commitments to gender equality can be viewed in the global policy making arena. In recent years, international and state-level policy agendas such as the suite of UN Security Council Women, Peace and Security Resolutions (hereafter WPS), which aim to highlight the disproportionate effect of conflict on women, and the labelling of foreign policy as feminist by countries such as Sweden and Canada indicate a normalisation of, and at least, rhetorical commitment to some aspects of women's rights. Whether these policies are successful in their implementation or go beyond rhetorical commitment has of course been open to academic critique. These international policies have particular relevance in NI. The WPS resolutions have been embraced by the women's and community sector to highlight the under-representation of women in peacebuilding and as discussed in Chapter 4 have, with regard to participation in decision making, been translated and vernaculized successfully in the local context.

At the same time, well financed and coordinated global far-right movements protest against what they describe as 'gender ideology'. This backlash against social and political change has been argued to be successful in global policy making and decision forums such as the UN (Cupać and Ebetürk, 2020), at national levels such as the rollback on abortion rights witnessed in the United States and Poland and in the rise of men's rights groups who argue that their rights (particularly in the family) are being eroded by the progression of women's rights (Dragiewicz, 2008). Anti-feminist alliances rely on arguments about the restoration of traditional, conservative family units and gender roles, suggesting a regression or reversion in terms of political and social transformation, back to a time of stability that they perceive to have existed before second-wave feminism. These arguments travel transnationally through social media, the rise of social media masculinity 'influencers' and what is termed the 'manosphere', having tangible impacts on men's behaviour and attitudes towards women and girls (Roberts and Wescott, 2024; Dickel and Evolvi, 2023).

Debates about 'gender ideology' go beyond those who are anti-feminist. Within feminist groups, there is a toxic debate about the commitment of some feminists to the sex/gender binary and the use of this to exclude trans women from feminist or 'women only' space or to acknowledge their existence at all (Phipps, 2020). This has led some feminists to forge 'unholy alliances' with far-right groups who argue against the progression of women's rights and rights for those from gender and sexual minorities.

Localised feminist movements working on social, political and gender transformations of course work within these global frameworks and tensions but also within the historical legacies of their particular context. For feminists in NI, this is a legacy of violent conflict and separation of communities based on sectarianism. Feminist approaches to conflict and peace have highlighted the false assumption that a transition from violent conflict to peace means an end to violence for all, and that in fact the value placed on political stability may exclude particular groups of people and marginalise certain social justice issues. However, it has also been noted that conflicts can have a potentially liberating effect on women, with the opening of 'intended and unintended spaces for empowering women, effecting structural and social transformations and producing new social, economic and political realities that redefine gender and caste hierarchies' (Machanda, 2001: 4). Such situations offer the potential to disrupt and challenge gender orders and make women's inequality more visible. However, it is widely recognised that women's contributions are regularly marginalised and minimised in the aftermath of conflict (Meintjes et al., 2001). This is often accompanied by a return to the pre-conflict gender order and the reintegration of women in the private sphere (Nikolic-Ristanovic, 2002). In these scenarios, similar to the gender backlash described above, political stability is seen to be achieved by reverting to conservative or traditional gender roles.

In societies moving out of conflict, women engage and are active in movements for justice, the enforcement of human rights norms, institutional reform and the provision of security, yet 'they generally rely on structures that do not encourage them to think about the manifold ways in which they have been victimized' (Rubio-Marín, 2006: 22). Many post-conflict societies notably lack gender-sensitive mechanisms for interpreting and addressing the structural harms and inequalities which particularly affect women. Ní Aoláin argues 'the matters that are framed as central issues for resolution in transitional negotiations may only peripherally impact many women's day-to-day lives' (Ní Aoláin, 2006: 831). Within the NI peace agreement, the participation of the Northern Ireland Women's Coalition (NIWC) ensured that women's right to political participation was contained within the Agreement but there was no mechanism introduced to ensure fulfilment. Institutional innovations such as the Civic Forum which was designed to ensure the voice of civil society in policymaking could have also facilitated women's inclusion and representation, yet quickly fell by the wayside and are yet to be re-established (see Chapter 1 for further discussion of the NIWC).

Public, political spaces have long been male-dominated due to the artificial public/private divide which was 'constructed through the exclusion of women and all that we symbolize' (Pateman, 1989: 52). Whilst political spaces and discourses are shaped through the bodies that they exclude, this does not mean that these spaces are fixed or unresponsive in the face of change (Puwar, 2004). In fact, space 'moves and changes, depending on how it is used, what is done with and to it, and how open it is to even further changes' (Grosz, 2001: 7). Whilst there remains no legal impediment to women's political participation, there are certain bodies that are perceived to belong in certain spaces and others that are marked as trespassing (Puwar, 2004). Contemporary features of political institutions that illustrate this symbolic exclusion include modes of debate, unwritten cultural norms, sexist treatment and language used to describe women in politics and the specific violences that women are more likely to experience including online and sexual harassment. In Northern Ireland, governance is formed through power-sharing which has been critiqued from a gender perspective (Byrne and McCulloch, 2012; Kennedy et al., 2016; Pierson and Thomson, 2018) as entrenching particular conservative ethno-national understandings of gender identity and marginalising gendered policy concerns such as abortion and same-sex marriage (see the following chapter for more detail) yet it remains important to interrogate these spaces as sites of potential transformation.

Particular conservative notions of gender and the primacy of ethno-national politics have also ensured the exclusion of gendered concerns from broader public political discussions in Northern Ireland. Habermas's idea of the public sphere, defined as 'a discursive space in which individuals and groups associate to discuss matters of mutual interest and, where possible, to reach a common judgment about them' (Hauser, 1998: 61), has been critiqued by feminist scholars (most notably Nancy Fraser) for its lack of consideration of parity of participation, in particular by socially marginalised groups. However, groups that have historically been socially and politically subordinated have not waited on their inclusion in dominant institutions but set up separate political spaces and discursive arenas, termed by Nancy Fraser (1999) as subaltern counterpublics. These counterpublics are spaces where members can formulate their interests, identities and needs on their own terms and in their own language. Whilst they can function as separate spaces, they can also interact and agitate against wider publics. This is where, Fraser argues, their emancipatory potential arises. Fraser uses the example of the women's movement and its ability to make domestic violence a common concern and an issue of political priority rather than a minority private sphere issue. This ability to formulate and articulate concerns indicates the strength of multiple political arenas in terms of parity of participation and as a counter to state power. I consider feminist groups and more broadly the women's sector[1] in NI as subaltern counterpublics through their exclusion from dominant political discourse, however, I will examine their ability to articulate and translate their arguments and ideas to the broader public and formal political realm as a means of shifting gender stereotypes and political space.

There is of course the question of broader political change and where feminism sits within this. The future status of Northern Ireland may involve changes ranging from reform of the Assembly to constitutional change on the island of Ireland. These questions have engaged a range of positions in recent years. Whatever future systems of governance look like in Northern Ireland need to engage feminist actors and integrate a gender lens. This will involve difficult conversations between feminists but is vitally necessary to ensure that broader political shifts and changes are not made without the perspectives, experiences and voices of women included.

Interrogating feminist and gender politics in any terrain brings up the plurality of feminisms. What a policy maker may describe as feminist will most likely be very different to what a grassroots activist believes to be feminist. Commitments to gender equality in global and state forums has largely been described as commitments to liberal notions of feminism and equality and this can come into tension with the more radical goals and strategies of feminist activist groups. Rather than dismissing relationships between different visions of feminism it is productive to examine the tensions in these relationships to look for points of commonality or where ideas shift through dialogue. I am not proposing that one form of feminism has more potential to transform gender power relations than another but that in examining different approaches we may begin to find glimpses of transformative change.

Background to the research and research questions

This book explores contemporary feminist politics and organising and its contribution to transforming political space and gender identities in Northern Ireland. It focuses on the following questions:

- How does feminist organising in a post-conflict society fit within the framework of contemporary feminism?
- How do feminist actors make use of different political spaces to advance feminist agendas?
- To what extent do legacies of the past impact on gender identities and equality in the present?
- Can feminist politics beyond the state be a means to reshape dominant political identities and discourses?

When developing the core arguments and thematic structure of this book, I took as a starting point that there is political and social importance in concerns and activities that are thought of as outside the realm of formal, electoral politics. In this way, whilst I acknowledge that feminist political transformation could happen within the Assembly and through electoral politics, it is only one site of politics engaged with in the book. Political and social change can occur through actions deliberately taken beyond the state (be that via external bodies or through social movements) and through everyday interactions. During 2022 and 2023, I undertook approximately thirty interviews with activists, women's and community sector representatives, academics and elected representatives identified as key political actors in feminist transformation. They were asked about the spaces they believed to be most facilitative to such change in Northern Ireland, the barriers and opportunities that existed to achieve change, the most effective discourses and framings of feminism and gender equality and how their work specifically fitted into this change. The interviews were conducted online and ranged from between fifty minutes to over two hours.

All of those who took part in interviews identified as women or non-binary. Whilst those from the trans community were invited to participate, it is acknowledged as a limitation of this book that there were no transgender participants (whilst trans rights were discussed by participants this of course reflect their perception). Similarly, with regard to race, only one participant worked in an organisation focussing on racial equality. These interviews helped me to gain a broader appreciation of how the individuals and groups involved in change defined, framed and understood ideas of feminist transformation in their own language, and these rich conversations helped to uncover processes and instances of change in addition to ongoing challenges and sticking points in furthering gender equality and feminist goals.

Whilst data was collected specifically for this book, the book is the product of a much longer research trajectory. I have previously written on feminist activism in NI (Deiana and Pierson, 2015; Pierson, 2017; Pierson et al., 2022) and conducted research on the women's sector and implementation of WPS Resolutions for the NI Community Relations Council in 2016 (Pierson and Radford, 2016). Whilst my focus has not been on women's descriptive representation in the Assembly, I have written on the gendered considerations of power-sharing (Kennedy et al., 2016; Pierson and Thomson, 2018). Since 2016 my research has largely focused on abortion and within the NI context I have written on political discourse on abortion and activist and civil society framings on abortion rights (Pierson and Bloomer, 2017; Bloomer et al., 2018). I have also been part of projects researching abortion rights in the workplace (Bloomer et al., 2023) and Female Genital Cutting (FGC) and policy response (MacNamara et al., 2020). These projects helped inform the research themes and questions for this book.

As a feminist reflexive researcher (Wasserfall, 1993) it is important to acknowledge my own background in the research. In addition to academic research, I have been and continue to be part of the feminist activist community in NI. From 2010 to 2011 I worked for Women's News Magazine providing training to schools in north Belfast on women and the media and have been involved in Belfast Feminist Network in its early years. Currently, I am Chair of the Board of Alliance for Choice Belfast, one of the organisations integral to the campaign for abortion rights in NI. Since 2017, I have lived in England and therefore am not as embedded within the feminist community which could be argued as a strength for a researcher as there is a level of critical distance which enables analysis. It may also be read as a weakness as I am not as able to engage in the daily observation of movement building and change. This experience is important to my interpretation of the data collected for the project. The data was analysed using reflexive thematic analysis (Braun and Clarke, 2006; 2021). Reflexive thematic analysis allows the researcher to use their experience as part of the coding process rather than attempting to remain 'outside' or 'unbiased' in developing themes from their data.

It is also important to note that there is an immense amount of research and literature which has been developed by the women's and community sector over the last twenty years and I have made use of this throughout the text. Organisations such as the Women's Resource and Development Agency[2] (WRDA), the Women's Support Network[3] (WSN), the Women's Platform[4] (formerly the Northern Ireland Women's European Network) and the Training for Women Network[5] (TWN) have produced a range of outputs which when brought together help to trace a history of gender inequality and identify ongoing challenges (such as domestic violence or the impact of austerity) to issues which have achieved substantive change (such as abortion rights). These documents illustrate the framings the women's sector have taken on particular issues, how they have been vernacularized for different audiences and unfortunately quite often how much work still remains to be done to transform gender relations in NI. These documents provide an important resource indicating how the women's sector conceptualises gender equality. Institutional reports such as the CEDAW optional protocol inquiry into NI's abortion laws, WPS National Action Plans of the UK and Irish governments and reports on gender equality produced by the NI Assembly also provide a contextualisation of issues.

The terminology within this book has been chosen for accuracy rather than political motivation. I predominantly use the term Northern Ireland as it describes the political and legal jurisdiction within which laws and policies are made. I recognise that many of those interviewed for this book see their activism as part of a wider Irish feminism and in quotes use their language and expression. With regard to language around sexuality, I use the term LGBT+ to recognise a range of positions that may, but do not always, identify with LGBT+ acronym. This includes but is not limited to non-binary, asexual and intersex people. The term 'woman' when used, is intended to be inclusive to anyone who identifies as a woman.

The social and political context of Northern Ireland

To understand the context within which feminists work it is first necessary to outline the particular context of Norther Ireland. In Chapter 1 there is a more detailed account of gender politics in the region, whereas this section provides a brief outline of the mainstream historical, social and political context.

Terminology is important within explanations of Northern Ireland, whether the events of Northern Ireland between 1969 and 1994 are defined as a conflict, a war or criminal acts are seen to determine the resulting analysis of these events. There are multiple disagreements over the type of conflict that took place, the 'conflict over the conflict' (McGarry and O'Leary, 1995) and the UK government has carefully avoided referring to the situation in

Northern Ireland as an 'armed conflict'. However, it is increasingly accepted that between 1969 and 1994 a degree of political violence took place which reached the level of armed conflict (Ní Aoláin, 2000). This terminological impasse extends to the term 'post-conflict', due to the blurring of lines between conflict and transitional environments. These terms are used in highly politicised ways and shed light on certain issues while downplaying others (Vaughn-Williams, 2006).

Groups in Northern Ireland have often been referred to by their religious identity whilst in fact conflict has predominantly revolved around the constitutional status of Northern Ireland (Mitchell, 2006). Put simply, Nationalists (mainly Catholic) want Northern Ireland to unify with the twenty-six counties of the Republic of Ireland via peaceful means whilst Republicans have advocated armed struggle to achieve unity. Unionists (mainly Protestant) want Northern Ireland to remain part of the United Kingdom whilst Loyalist identity has more militant links in defence of the (British) union and opposition to Irish unity. Obviously, identities are not always as rigidly defined as described above and there are nuances and evolutions within these descriptions, for example, recent studies have pointed towards an emerging 'Northern Irish' identity. The 2021 Northern Ireland Life and Times Survey indicated that 27 per cent of people described themselves as British, 32 per cent as Irish and 31 per cent as Northern Irish.[6]

Historical inequalities between Catholic and Protestant communities came from three predominant sources; the gerrymandering of local council constituency borders to facilitate a Unionist majority vote, the allocation of public housing and the high level of unemployment (in the early 1960s Catholic unemployment stood at 14 per cent whilst Protestant unemployment stood at 6 per cent) (Edwards and McGratten, 2010). It has been pointed out that class was also an integral factor in inequality. The right to vote (in local council elections) was only granted to ratepayers and their spouses, therefore almost 25 per cent of people did not have the right to vote, also affecting Protestants from socio-economically poorer backgrounds (Keenan-Thomson, 2010).

The creation of the Northern Ireland Civil Rights Association in the 1960s prompted mass civil rights marches in the 1960s calling for reforms. The prospect of reforms served to entrench political identities, with Unionists deeming them unsettling and for many Nationalists being too little too late (Keenan-Thomson, 2010). In addition, the militant policing of these marches coupled with Loyalist counter demonstrations and violence (often by off-duty part-time reserve police officers) increased disillusionment and positioned policing as a contentious issue (Dixon and O'Kane, 2011). The re-emergence of paramilitary organisations, notably the Provisional IRA on the Republican side and the Ulster Volunteer Force (UVF) and Ulster

Defence Association (UDA) on the Loyalist side, polarised ideologies and began a militaristic campaign on one side to end partition and on the other to maintain it. In response to increasing violence and reprisals between Republican and Loyalist organisations, the British government suspended the Northern Ireland (Stormont) government and implemented direct rule in 1972. This was viewed as a temporary measure, yet as with many policies implemented in Northern Ireland, in fact ended up lasting for over a quarter of a century. The British government attempted to frame the dimensions of the conflict within law-and-order terms, denying the political dimensions and acting accordingly to 'contain' violence (Ní Aoláin, 2000).

Formal political efforts to resolve the conflict were attempted, most notably through the implementation of power-sharing in the 1973 Sunningdale Agreement (which was substantively similar to the Good Friday Agreement) and the Anglo-Irish Agreement (AIA) in 1985 which recognised the right of the Irish government to be consulted by Britain over Northern Ireland. However, these in fact heightened antagonisms and sparked province-wide strikes and violence (McGarry and O'Leary, 1995). The strikes highlighted Unionist disagreement with political agreements viewed as increasing Irish government power over Northern Ireland politics and the road to Irish unity. The situation post-AIA period appeared to be one of stagnant and irretractable conflict yet discussions behind the scenes were leading to the paramilitary ceasefires and peace negotiations in the 1990s (Dixon and O'Kane, 2011). The Downing Street Declaration in 1993 (Joint Declaration for Peace) and the 1994 paramilitary ceasefires initiated the possibility of a more substantive peace agreement (Tonge, 2002). Elections to the Northern Ireland Forum were complex yet designed to allow smaller (predominantly Loyalist) parties to engage, as discussed in the next chapter this enabled the Northern Ireland Women's Coalition (NIWC) to get elected. The multi-party talks between 1996 and 1998 culminated in the Agreement.

The Agreement contains three core strands. Strand One created a consociational style system of governance with an Assembly of 108 seats and a cross-community Executive.[7] Strand Two established a North–South Ministerial Council and Strand Three formed a British–Irish Council with representatives from the British and Irish governments. The Agreement continues to affirm the right to self-determination for the citizens of Northern Ireland, incorporated the European Convention on Human Rights into Northern Ireland law, established a Civic Forum for consultation with civil society and permitted the release of political prisoners within two years (Wilford, 2010). The issue of policing was considered and agreed on the establishment of an independent commission. The Independent Commission on Policing for Northern Ireland consisted of eight members, only two were female.[8] In the Commission's report of 1999 (commonly referred to as the

Patten Report), 175 recommendations were made for the restructuring of the police service, one of the most significant being parity of employment between Catholic and Protestant communities. In 2001, the Royal Ulster Constabulary became the Police Service of Northern Ireland. Whilst parity in the make-up of the police force was considered from a religious perspective, no legislative quota was put in place to ensure gender parity. It was reasoned in the Patten report that as gender imbalance was an issue for all police forces it would not be subject to any affirmative action (Patten Report, 1999).

In the post-Agreement landscape, a shift can be seen in party dominance. At the time of the Agreement, the Ulster Unionist Party (UUP) and the Social Democratic and Labour Party (SDLP) held the majority of votes for their respective communities. Both parties were considered the more moderate proponents of Unionism and Nationalism respectively. Since then, there has been a rise in what can be called 'ethnic hardliners' Sinn Féin and the Democratic Unionist Party (DUP). Sinn Féin's rise in popularity has been attributed to its ability to make inroads into middle class, conservative Catholic communities and the DUP's success due to its connection to communities (Thomson, 2016). Both parties have a strong leadership and party structure. The success of these parties can also be looked at through the framework of consociationalism where academic criticism has pointed to the embedding of identity through this particular form of governance. However, more recently the Alliance Party has seen its vote share increase, in the 2019 elections they held 16 per cent of the vote share, contrasting with an average of 7 per cent between 1974 and 2016 (Tonge, 2020). The Alliance party claims neutrality on the position of (Northern) Ireland's constitutional future and appeals to voters who also do not identify as either Unionist or Nationalist. In this way, they represent a growing group of people who may be less invested in constitutional politics.

The Assembly itself since the Agreement has only functioned for limited periods of time and can be characterised by its instability. There have been five suspensions of the NI Assembly, lasting from one day to four years and at the time of writing the devolved administration has only just reformed. At times the Assembly has not functioned because it has been suspended by the British government (as between 2002 and 2006), and at others because parties have refused to share power (as in 2022 and 2017) (Haughey, 2023). During these periods direct rule from Westminster is implemented or limited form of civil service rule (where officials take over responsibility for running public services). Neither of these options is democratically or constitutionally appealing with direct rule policies failing to respond to local needs and civil service rule legally and financially uncertain (Horgan, 2006; Haughey, 2023). As Sinn Féin are now the largest party in the Assembly since the

May 2022 elections, they take the position of First Minister. Recent political instability resulted from the DUP's refusal to nominate a Deputy First Minister, their intransience over UK–EU post-Brexit trading agreements and opposition to any border in the Irish Sea. After the Safeguarding the Union[9] report was published by the British government the Assembly was restored in February 2024 with Sinn Féin's Michelle O'Neill as First Minister and the DUP's Emma Little-Pengelly as Deputy First Minister.

Structure of the book

This book sets out to provide a unique analysis of feminist movement building and transformation of gender relations within a society coming out of violent conflict and one which is deemed to be constitutionally unsettled. Its relevance will be primarily for those working on the politics of Northern Ireland or specifically on the gender politics of Northern Ireland. However, the themes of the book mean it is situated within contemporary feminist thought and therefore will contribute to the examination of fourth wave feminism or contemporary feminist movement building and because of the location and political situation, useful, for anyone interrogating gender relations and equality in societies emerging from violent conflict or crisis.

Moving on from the introduction, Chapter 1 sets out the gender order of Northern Ireland. Using literature on the region, it examines gender as part of dominant ethno-national identities and as embedded in institutions, addressing how this has affected women's political activity and activism. Gender is not treated as a fixed construct but a socially, historically and politically situated concept and one which is open to change and evolution. Through this chapter, we can see how women's political activity has developed within the particular constraints of the region and the impact of this on attitudes to gender equality.

Having set up a framework for analysis, Chapter 2 moves to consider feminist movement building in NI. After providing a history of activism in the province it uses identified aspects of fourth wave feminism including intersectionality, networks and coalition building and social media to analyse how collective voices and agendas are built and maintained. Chapter 3 then considers feminist engagement with the state in the form of gender experts, those who provide evidence and expertise for policymakers working outside the state, in particular in the women's sector. The chapter identifies that while the women's sector has created a legitimate voice in formal political spaces, challenges remain in terms of translating and vernacularizing feminist goals in spaces where gender equality is interpreted in a formal sense. The slowness of change in NI, often impeded by the regular crises in the Assembly creates a frustrating situation for those attempting to influence policy.

With the lack of importance given to gender policy issues within formal politics and the periods of stalled devolution, feminist actors have often turned to external mechanisms to further their goals. The CEDAW optional protocol inquiry is one successful example of this and the use of the UN Security Council Resolutions on Women, Peace and Security to frame requests for the inclusion of women in peacebuilding is another example with mixed results. Chapter 4 considers silences on gender-based violence in the past and its link to contemporary justice and masculinities. Whilst the WPS resolutions have gained great traction in the region and have been successfully translated into local goals, they have been framed around participation rather than to begin an investigation into the historical legacies of GBV, their link to conflict and their relation to contemporary GBV and gender relations. This chapter concludes that peace cannot be built solely on the inclusion of women but must consider GBV in the past and present to begin a process of transforming gender relations.

Finally, Chapter 5 uses the framework of prefigurative politics to examine abortion rights activism before and after legal change. The chapter argues that the care provided by activists to those seeking abortion provides a glimpse of potential political and gender transformation through its expansive notion of who we should care for and about. Societies defined by sectarianism can draw tight boundaries around communities and who we should care for and about, expanding the notion of care and caring for others can begin the process of redrawing or eradicating these boundaries helping us to envision different political spaces and ways of doing politics.

The concluding chapter summarises the books main findings and draws together the themes to interrogate the ways in which feminist and gender actors have challenged and changed the dominant gender order and made inroads to gender transformations.

Notes

1 The women's sector includes voluntary and community groups specifically set up for women and umbrella groups created to coordinate the sector. These groups are discussed in more depth in the following chapter and in Chapter 3.
2 https://wrda.net/ (last accessed 12/02/2025).
3 https://www.communityni.org/organisation/womens-support-network-0 (last accessed 12/02/2025).
4 https://womensplatform.org/ (last accessed 12/02/2025).
5 https://www.twnonline.com/ (last accessed 12/02/2025).

6 Find results here: https://www.ark.ac.uk/nilt/2021/Community_Relations/NINATID.html (last accessed 12/02/2025).
7 The Fresh Start Agreement 2015 reduces the number of Assembly members from 108 to 90. Access here: https://assets.publishing.service.gov.uk/media/5a80a8a5e5274a2e8ab516ce/A_Fresh_Start_-_The_Stormont_Agreement_and_Implementation_Plan_-_Final_Version_20_Nov_2015_for_PDF.pdf (last accessed 12/02/2025).
8 Chaired by Conservative politician Chris Patten, the other members of the Commission were Maurice Hayes, Peter Smith, Kathleen O'Toole, Gerald W. Lynch, Sir John Smith, Lucy Woods and Professor Clifford Shearing.
9 https://assets.publishing.service.gov.uk/media/65ba3b7bee7d490013984a59/Command_Paper__1_.pdf (last accessed 12/02/2025).

1

Gender identities and political spaces

Gender, whilst often portrayed as of peripheral importance to the operation of politics, is an integral mechanism dictating both access to, and the ability to shape, political spaces. Before examining the ways in which feminist actors have integrated into existing political spaces and created new ones, it is important to interrogate dominant constructions of gender and how gender shapes and controls political spheres. The primary framing of politics and identity in Northern Ireland is through the lens of violent conflict and its relationship to ethno-national identities. Gender is baked into these identity constructions, with specific roles being allocated to men and women. Linking femininity and masculinity to specific societal roles shapes who is viewed to be a legitimate political actor and which voices get heard in political discussions. Theresa O'Keeffe (2012: 85) writes that in the Northern Ireland context there is 'a kind of complex and ambivalent acceptance of dominant categories and practices', highlighting that whilst women may act politically this may not challenge the prevailing gender order.

Gender and ethno-national identities, as well as mapping onto individual bodies and collective identities, are built into structures and institutions of governance arising out of the Agreement and continue to shape political and social life. The lack of inclusion of women and gendered concerns in peace processes and agreements has been well documented and has effects on the likely success of such agreements (O'Reilly et al., 2015). This supposed gender-neutrality in political processes continues to place men as dominant and legitimate political actors. The primacy of ethno-national identity in institutions set up under the framework of consociationalism has been identified by feminist researchers to impede the advancement of gender issues on the political agenda (Kennedy et al., 2016). Whilst women may face no particular barriers to being elected under power-sharing, substantive representation of women is constrained. These constraints have tangible impacts on how feminist actors interact with political institutions and how they create and shape space outside formal politics. This chapter gives an account of gender, its relationship to ethno-national identity, its inclusion within the political structures of Northern Ireland and the constraints it puts on women's political activity. In this way, it frames the following chapters of the book and provides the context from within which feminist actors work politically.

Gender and ethno-national identities

Every society has a particular gender order. How we understand femininities and masculinities and their relationship to politics is structurally and discursively constructed and therefore unfixed (despite how fixed it may feel) and open to change. Northern Ireland is noted to have a particularly conservative gender order, often explained via its strong infusion of ethno-national and religious identities. The construction of ethno-national identities has been explored by feminist academics and revealed to be a highly gendered process (Yuval-Davis, 1993). The development of the nation, whether it is viewed as an historical invention or an imagined community (Day and Thomson, 2004), is dependent on shared experience, history and memory deriving from a collective past of masculinised memory and hope (Enloe cited in McClintock, 1993). This shared history is constructed around specific roles being assigned to men and women and highly institutionalised gender differences transmitting power and property to males. Women are seen to 'bear the brunt' of this form of identity politics in terms of their range of life choices (Imam and Yuval-Davis, 2004).

Although nationalism is not a static concept often women's role in the development of the nation is as living history (McClintock, 1993). Women more often than men are compelled to inhabit traditional roles and their power is symbolic rather than in direct national agency as witnessed through the role of the male citizen-soldier (Fraser, 2013). Women's connection to national identity is often presumed to be 'weaker' than men's allowing for some to argue that women are more able to transcend identity. Floya Anthias and Nira Yuval-Davis have identified the ways women are employed in nationalism, primarily in the role as a mother and reproducer of cultural norms (1989). The act of mothering is used as a tool to biologically reproduce the culture, language, traditions and myths of the nation in its children. Women may also reproduce cultural and moral norms through restrictions on, and the policing of, sexual conduct. Theorists suggest that the role of women as supporters of nationalism positions them as passive bystanders and thus less connected to the active construction of national identities (McClintock, 1993).

Gender identity operates on binaries and subsequent hierarchies. In conflict situations, whilst men are positioned as active and viewed to be naturally involved in politics and political violence through the role of the citizen-soldier, women are situated as passive bystanders and inherently peaceful through their role as mothers. This link between mothering and peace can be seen in the Northern Ireland context in particular through peace movements led by women in the 1970s. Women Together was a cross-community movement which began in 1970 in small groups organising across Northern Ireland, their work was focused on practical grassroots peace building often done in secret (Carr, 2014). The better-known Peace People was created in 1976 by Betty Williams and Mairead Corrigan who won the Nobel Peace Prize in the same year. The group was started after the death of Corrigan's sister's children who were hit by a car driven by an IRA member pursued by British soldiers in West Belfast. Motivations for setting up women-centred peace movements are often described as developing from the context of raising children in a violent society and enabling women's experiences to be heard in male-dominated and militarised environments. Peace groups were often criticised for remaining neutral on constitutional issues or for calling for an end to violence without engaging with the roots of violence, however, their work was integral to provide space for the engagement of people across community divides in incredibly hostile and sometimes dangerous circumstances. In addition, these groups were often a starting point for women to develop a political voice. However, despite women's association with peace, they are often invisible within political processes, such as peace negotiations and leadership positions in formal and community-based peacebuilding.

In the context of Northern Ireland, conservative and nationalist ideals of the role of motherhood appeal to both traditions within Irish Nationalism and British Unionism (Ashe, 2006). Conservative Catholicism and evangelical Protestantism both revere and aim to uphold conservative gender roles. Within the perspective of Irish Nationalism, the concept of national territory as 'Mother Ireland' and the central figure of the Virgin Mary within Catholicism both posit ideals of womanhood as suffering self-sacrificing mothers. Whilst there is less evocative imagery of women within Protestant Unionist tradition, the Protestant churches draw sharp distinctions between male and female roles, implying strict moral codes surrounding women's sexuality and self-sacrificing nature for family and community. A common, yet contested, assumption is that women play a supporting rather than active role within Unionism (Ward, 2006). The elevation of motherhood has implications in positioning the role of women as helpers to political movements rather than actors and a particularly conservative view of women's sexuality and respectability. This both limits women's voices in politics and the ability to challenge gender norms and issues within political arenas. As Ashe (2006; 2007) has noted, motherhood provides a ready-made identity from which women can mobilise politically, but its remit is limited in terms of how much it can challenge conservative gender roles.

An example of the limitations of political mobilisation of conservative gender roles can be exemplified through the almost complete ban on abortion which lasted until 2019. Until relatively recently there has been limited activism in Northern Ireland on abortion rights with many women's groups taking a neutral position on the issue or remaining silent about it (Pierson and Bloomer, 2017). This stance was often due to a fear of backlash or controversy or based on personal positions on the issue. Abortion and its implicit rejection of motherhood crosses boundaries of ideal womanhood and self-sacrificing motherhood and as such does not fit within an acceptable political ethno-national identity for women (Pierson, 2018a). Of course, this ideological position does not match the reality of women's experiences with approximately one thousand women per year (from across the two dominant ethno-national groups) travelling to England to access abortion care prior to the legal change (Bloomer and Hoggart, 2016). However, the difficulty of achieving vocal support across the spectrum of women's and human rights groups for so long illustrates the strength of conservative gender ideology.

Theory on masculinities has illustrated the traits that are perceived to be those of 'real' men or dominant masculinities (Connell, 1995). Dominant traits of masculinity often refer to a capacity for strength and violence. Whilst there are multiple understandings of masculinity it has been theorised that some of the most powerful ideals of masculinity are that of the male-warrior and those constructed during war and processes of militarisation (Dowler, 2002; Nagel, 1999). Whilst dominant accounts of conflict and politics centre men's experiences, there is less literature theorising masculinities in Northern Ireland. Northern Ireland has been referred to as an 'armed patriarchy' highlighting the militarised form of masculinity viewed to dominate male identities. In conflict, the emasculation of the nation and protection of its women and children is often evoked as a reason to engage in militarised action. For example, concern over the feminisation of the Irish nation through British colonialism conflates with the rise in violence as a return to manhood for Irish men (Ashe, 2012). For Unionist and Loyalist men, the role of defenders of the community could be exercised through either joining the Royal Ulster Constabulary or a paramilitary organisation (Bairner, 1999). The Troubles reinforced men's power in the public and private sphere and held in place militarised forms of masculinity (Ashe and Harland, 2014).

As a socially constructed identity, masculinities can be reinforced or reconstituted; questioning dominant forms of masculinity is an important process in considering power and gender relations in a transforming society where gender stereotypes and marginalisation continue. Within the peace context, the male defender/protector role occupied by paramilitaries within communities have been transformed to some extent into community leadership and representative roles. As community and peace building work has become more formalised and funded, it has turned into a profession. These jobs then became an option for ex-political prisoners who were released under the conditions of the Agreement. Women have noted the retraction of space in community spheres for women to take an active and visible role and the dominance of men as gatekeepers to communities (Pierson, 2019). Gatekeepers will be those seen to lead communities and therefore those who will have access to political power to define community needs, divest funding and shape the discourse around community building and peace work. This gatekeeping of women's organising constrains the type of activities they can engage in and the stances they can take on issues. In some circumstances, women have had to meet outside their community to engage in conversations freely on issues of peace, culture and parading (Pierson, 2015). The conflation of ex-political prisoners and paramilitaries with community leadership roles contributes to the continued marginalisation of women and reverence towards militarised masculinity (Ashe, 2019b).

There have been other occasions where women's centres have been taken over by or threatened by paramilitary actors (Pierson, 2015). This is similar to incidences which happened during the conflict (Cockburn, 1998). This control can be embedded and strengthened through processes designed to transition paramilitary actors to community politics. The Tackling Paramilitarism Programme is a policy designed to support the transition of paramilitary groups toward community-development, restorative justice and conflict-transformation practices. It arose from the Fresh Start Agreement in 2015 and its commitment to tackle paramilitary activity and organised crime. However, it has been argued that the policy may also act to legitimise and rebrand the continuance of paramilitary dominance and activity simply under another name (Turner and Swaine, 2021). In the face of funding cuts and political and paramilitary blockages, women's centres have continued to provide vital spaces for women who continue to be affected by legacies of violence.

Paramilitarism is not only a problem of the past and highlights the strength of militarised visions of masculinity. The role of paramilitaries is still resonant and desirable for some young men especially in communities with low levels of educational attainment and high unemployment (Jarman, 2008). The promise of power that comes with paramilitarism is a lure to many young men who seek the perceived glory of the past (McDowell, 2008). In Republican communities the sustained impact of paramilitarism can be viewed through the rise in support for dissidents (Topping and Byrne, 2012) and is exemplified in Loyalist communities in the ease with which younger Loyalists have engaged in rioting around disputes about parading and the removal of the Union flag from being flown daily from the City Hall in Belfast (Ashe and Harland, 2014). Young men and women are also victims of ongoing paramilitary violence and intimidation, with gendered aspects to this violence including the use of sexual violence against women (McAlister et al., 2022).

It is important to note that the identities described above also rest on the premise of heteronormativity. Societies with strong ethno-national identities have been found to have prevalent and pervasive homophobia (Nagel, 1999). Gender identities are heavily correlated with sexuality and the use of gendered bodies in pursuit of the growth and defence of the nation. Women's role as mothers biologically reproducing the nation and men's as soldier defenders plays on historical exclusions of LGBT+ populations from these roles and renders their identities redundant in the pursuit of the national project (Ashe, 2019a). In other cases, sexual minorities can be framed as threats to the national project and bodies violently policed if they deviate from perceived sexual norms. Homosexuality was not decriminalised in Northern Ireland until 1982, and gay people were targeted by the police (and sometimes by paramilitary groups) (Ashe, 2019a). There were concerns that sexual minorities could be targeted by the security forces to coerce them into becoming informants. Politicians, such as the Rev. Ian Paisley (founder of the DUP), openly opposed the decriminalisation of homosexuality, creating the 'Save Ulster from Sodomy' campaign in the late 1970s. The targeting of LGBT+ populations in conflict is an emerging area of research and the visible inclusion of sexual minorities in agreements and transitions from conflict is largely confined to formal equality provisions.

Challenging gender identities

Whilst gendered ethno-national identities promote specific roles and behaviours for men and women this does not mean that these are accepted or strictly followed. Situations of war and conflict have been theorised as providing increased space for gender roles to be challenged by women. Conflicts can open up spaces for women to challenge and potentially transcend traditional gender orders, but it is also widely recognised that women's contributions are regularly marginalised and minimised in the aftermath of conflict (Meintjes et al., 2001). This is accompanied by a return to the 'normality' of the pre-conflict gender order and the reintegration of women in the private sphere.

Begoña Aretxaga details the emergence of women into political activism, particularly from Nationalist and Republican communities in West Belfast in the 1970s, as a result of the Falls Road curfew and internment without trial (Aretxaga, 1997). These acts triggered the mass mobilisation of women who challenged curfews and established an alarm system to warn their community of the presence of the British army. This activism has been labelled 'accidental' due to the fact that women organised out of necessity rather than prior political ideologies (McWilliams, 2002). However, this term underestimates the importance that these women had in maintaining a community infrastructure and providing leadership at a time of great political and social upheaval. The establishment of the alarm system also positioned certain women as providers of security in their communities. Activism grew from a will to protect homes, families and communities and blurred the boundaries between the public and private sphere for women. Stereotypical gender roles often made women's activism possible and ultimately more successful. For many women, activism borne out of experiences of conflict spurred an awareness of gender inequalities and an interest in community leadership roles. These new roles made many unwilling to go back to the role of being primarily a housewife and mother after the release of male partners from prison.

The role of women in Unionist and Loyalist communities has been subject to minimal research in comparison with Nationalist and Republican women. It is questionable whether space opened in the same way for Unionist and Loyalist women to participate in political mobilisation. The few studies that exist on these women tend to emphasise the role of women as aids to men's activities, and has described women's role within Unionism as 'tea and sandwich makers' (Cockburn, 1998). It has been argued that 'the generally conservative political ideology of unionism leaves little space for feminist reconstructions of Unionist identity and politics' (Racioppi and See, 2000: 22). In addition, feminism within the Northern Ireland context has often been connected with Irish Nationalism in part through its potential to question power relationships and destabilise gender stereotypes (Stapleton and Wilson, 2013). Ward's (2006) research on Unionist women and political participation challenges this view and illustrates the range of roles that women take on, albeit largely in a support capacity rather than a central visible political role. Ward argues that the increase of women in formal political roles may have little impact on gender policy decisions due to politicisation on the basis of national identity rather than gender. Nevertheless, although Unionist and Loyalist women's political mobilisation is under-documented there is some evidence to suggest some women challenged gender norms though cross community work on gender inequality (Davies et al., 2000).

Despite the predominant imagery of male combatants, women also became involved in the military campaigns of Republicanism and Loyalism. One in twenty of those imprisoned on political grounds between 1969 and 1998 were women (Potter and MacMillan, 2008). Female combatants present a challenge to traditional ideas about war, peace and gender roles; they also challenge notions of men being the predominant agents of protection and defence within communities (Alison, 2004). Women's involvement in Republicanism has been documented in more detail than their Loyalist counterparts. Women have been involved within armed Republicanism since the movement emerged; however, women were directed towards the women's branch of the IRA, *Cumann na mBan*. In the early 1970s some women expressed discontent at being 'slaves' to their male counterparts but as the decade progressed, IRA Council documents highlight the increased importance of women's role within the organisation (Talbot, 2004). At the time *Cumann na mBan* was dissolved and integrated into the wider IRA structure, the decision to include women more actively was partly strategic and partly due to women's insistence. In addition, the women who did join the IRA, although expressing an interest in feminism, held allegiance primarily to the national question.

Analysis of women's role within armed Republicanism has often focused on the experiences of women who were imprisoned. These women, through taking part in similar protests to male prisoners became more aware of their gendered experience and the conservative gender order within Republicanism and Northern Irish society as a whole (Corcoran, 2004). Female prisoners' decision to take part in the 'no wash' protests in 1980 and the hunger strikes of 1981 were taken in light of contrary advice from IRA leadership (Corcoran, 2004). The 'no wash' protests in particular brought to the fore women's different bodily experiences, as the notion of women having to menstruate without washing seemed particularly debasing to the male leadership. Women's possible commitment to hunger strikes was also doubted, calling into question the supposed limits to female political agency and commitment to ethno-national political ideology. Strip-searching which took place in Armagh Gaol (the primary women's prison) in the mid 1980s brought widespread international condemnation; to the imprisoned women it appeared that this form of humiliation was seen by the authorities to punish women who had been brought up in traditional Catholic households more effectively.

One of the most invisible and difficult to access groups is that of Loyalist female combatants. Researchers have noted that the perceived unfavourable view of Loyalist female paramilitaries within their communities has made them reluctant to be acknowledged (Potter and MacMillan, 2008). In addition, the role of male gatekeepers within Loyalist communities has made it difficult for researchers to access these women; in fact their existence has often been denied making it difficult to estimate how many of them exist. Miranda Alison cites a male Loyalist ex-prisoner as explaining women's supposed lack of involvement in paramilitary activity as a function of the different ideals of Loyalism and Republicanism. Republicanism was viewed (by this individual) as a revolutionary ideology whereas Loyalism was a reactionary and less cohesive movement (Alison, 2004). However, official statistics present 128 of the 2368 women imprisoned between 1969 and 2007 as having paramilitary affiliations with 20 per cent of these being affiliated to Loyalist organisations. Sandra McEvoy has documented that there were approximately three thousand women in the UDA and around 2 per cent of UVF membership were female (McEvoy, 2009).

McEvoy's research on Loyalist women active in paramilitary organisations illustrates the marginalisation of these women both within wider conflict narratives and their own communities. Interviews with female participants in Loyalist paramilitaries detail these women's motivations for joining paramilitary groups, showing that some felt a duty to protect their communities, their children and their country and also felt a sense of freedom, political agency and empowerment; a sense that their voices were being heard for the first time. These women have largely been excluded from the formal political and peacebuilding process and have found the agreements intended to bring peace to Northern Ireland problematic and objectionable. There is a tangible sense of disillusionment with political processes and agreements and being left behind by Unionist political parties.

More recently, there has been visible presence of Loyalist women in political protest. During protests in 2013 by Loyalists and Unionists over the removal of the Union Flag from Belfast City Hall, the number of women active in organising protests was noted in the media. Subsequent research on the issue has highlighted women's reasons for participating in these protests and noted that the Union Flag gave them 'a sense of security and allowed them to maintain the view that they had a place in the "new" Northern Ireland' (Byrne, 2013). Cultural identity provides a sense of belonging and ontological security and the perceived erosion and exclusion of Unionist and Loyalist identity feeds into discontent and disillusionment in the post-Agreement era.

Doing politics differently? Negotiating identity and transversal dialogue

Within divided societies how women organise and communicate has been theorised through the idea of transversal dialogue. This term was coined by Nira Yuval-Davis (2000) to refer to the creation of alliances between women with differing identities from distinct national communities. Yuval-Davis notes that transversal dialogue was introduced to her by Italian feminists in 1993 in the context of a meeting between Israeli and Palestinian women. Transversal politics is seen to encompass a process of 'rooting' and 'shifting' where participants remain rooted in their own community but who may shift into the positions of those from differing backgrounds, allowing for more empathy and communication within engagements. Such transversal politics is born out of material and practical concerns common to many women. Identity here is viewed to be heterogenous and mutable rather than fixed (Murtagh, 2008). Women are seen to work together despite differing identities to try to find common ground to tackle shared gender interests. Transversal dialogue encompasses both equality and difference and should involve actors who recognise and acknowledge their different social, economic and political power.

Within the Northern Ireland context, transversal politics was examined through Cynthia Cockburn's (1998) ethnographic work in the 1990s in the Women's Support Network, an alliance of Catholic, Protestant and mixed working-class women's groups in Belfast. Cockburn sees these relationships as built on common principles and objectives where participants engage in dialogue and debate to share knowledge and learn rather than attempt to take a unified stance. Elizabeth Porter (2000: 168) reflects on the risks that this work took arguing that the responsibility to risk creating dialogical spaces across difference is a strong one necessary for the creation of transformative politics. However, Cockburn found in her study of the Women's Support Network, that some members questioned the process, finding that the focus on small 'p' politics left areas of silence on harder issues of identity and politics. Transversal dialogue may also be described as a form of 'strategic essentialism' or a 'politics of avoidance', where identity is left aside for a period of time but of course has to be re-engaged with once participants are back in their own communities. Attempting to operate a politics of transversal dialogue may also render issues of gender inequality as outside of the political sphere. Rosemary Sales (1997) tells of how the administrator in a women's centre in a Protestant area told her, 'we don't talk about politics here. We only talk about women's issues' (1997: 169). This type of statement locates politics as being solely about constitutional issues and depoliticises gender concerns.

Theresa O'Keeffe (2021) terms this 'bridge-builder feminism', a blend of peace work and institutional feminism which sought to bridge ethnonational divides. This work is typified through a desire to break with past agnosticism on constitutional issues, a rejection of political violence and the acceptance of the legitimacy of the state. O'Keeffe argues that this ideal of prioritising gender or a universal sisterhood ignored intersectional identities and power structures and equated feminism with peacebuilding. As Eilish Rooney and Aisling Swaine (2012) have noted there is another side to transversal politics. The women's sector relies on funding from government to sustain itself and its activities. Funding structures can often be underpinned by taking part in cross-community activity. Whilst this work is important it may result in some women's groups eliding the intersectional inequality experienced by women on the basis of religious or political identity in order to remain fundable (Rooney and Swaine, 2012). Women working together across community divides can also be used strategically as a means to suggest progress and change. As such, engaging with knotty issues around identity may be discouraged, not as a means to facilitate dialogue but in order to maintain current structures. Minimising difference between women in this way may be to the detriment of those women living in communities which continue to be most affected by legacies of conflict.

Women who have been active in ethno-national movements and their experiences of inequality have often brought the critiques of transversal politics to the fore. In the 1980s, the women's movement was critiqued for ignoring the treatment of women prisoners in Armagh Gaol including the repeated strip searching by prison guards. Similarly, Robin Whitaker uses the example of the imprisonment of Roisin McAliskey as a key matter bringing issues of gender and ethno-national identity into tension within the Northern Ireland Women's Coalition (NIWC) (Whitaker, 2008). McAliskey (a Republican and the daughter of Bernadette Devlin McAliskey) was arrested in November 1996 under emergency anti-terrorism legislation whilst pregnant and because of her high-risk status was kept in solitary confinement with minimal time outside her cell. Although concern was expressed for McAliskey's health and pregnancy, because of her political affiliation it was challenging for some women in the NIWC to choose to support her as this support may have been read as validation for the wider Republican agenda. As highlighted by O'Keeffe (2021) a position which decries paramilitary violence but not state based gender violence has limitations in feminism. O'Keeffe points to Women's News (a feminist magazine based in Belfast) as an outlier as it began publishing more material on conflict related issues and printed letters and articles from women political prisoners in the latter half of the 1980s. Explicitly Republican feminist groups emerged at this time including Women Against Imperialism and *Clár na mBan*. Republican feminist discussions, detailed at the time of the peace process in a special edition of the Feminist Review in 1995, illustrate the tensions between questions of national identity and feminism. Claire Hackett puts this particularly well, 'the Republican feminist agenda is a thorn in the flesh of both the Republican and feminist movements in Ireland' (Hackett, 1995: 111). Hackett particularly highlights how women working together on reconciliation work can often be used as a means to suppress difference or a politics of avoidance. Republican feminism of this period also highlights that their support for the national question will not be unequivocal if not accompanied with wider transformation of gender roles (Connolly, 1995; Hackett, 1995).

Gender and peace agreements

Women's inclusion, or lack thereof, in peace processes is well documented. Women's participation in peace is often viewed through organising in more informal community-based initiatives which, while integral to grassroots peacebuilding, does not seem to translate into positions on peace negotiation teams and reinforces narratives of women building bridges and being conciliatory. There is a wealth of evidence which points to the importance of the inclusion of women in peace processes. Research undertaken by the Graduate Institute in Geneva has shown that in cases where women's groups were able to exercise a strong influence on peace negotiations, there was a much higher chance that agreement would be reached and implemented (O'Reilly et al., 2015). Quantitative analysis of 181 peace agreements signed between 1989 and 2011 showed that peace agreements which included women as signatories, witnesses, mediators and or/negotiators demonstrated a 20 per cent increase in probability of lasting at least two to ten years and a 35 per cent probability of lasting fifteen years (Stone, 2014). Peace agreements are 'a road map for a country's subsequent peace-building efforts' (Ellerby, 2013: 439) and have concrete effects on women in terms of who are considered legitimate actors in peacebuilding processes and who gets access to subsequent resources.

The Agreement negotiations have been noted as having higher visibility and presence of women than most (Pierson, 2018b). This is primarily based on the presence of the NIWC. The creation of the NIWC, as has been noted by its founders, was a reaction to the possibility that almost no women would be involved in the formal peace negotiations (Fearon, 1999). The party was composed mainly of women from academia, civil society and community politics with seventy candidates registered for election (Brown et al., 2002). The party was founded on the basis of representing women and grounded in principles of human rights and equality. Their neutral stance on constitutional issues however was publicly criticised by Republican women, who wrote an open letter stating that a woman's party that took a neutral stance on the constitutional position of Northern Ireland could not represent them (Little, 2002). Elections to the negotiations were structured in such a way to include more voices than the predominant political parties. However, in reality this was to include marginalised Loyalist perspectives rather than a wider section of society.

Benefitting from the electoral system to the Forum for Political Dialogue (set up as part of the negotiation process leading to the Agreement), the NIWC came ninth allowing them to send two participants to negotiations. These two women experienced first-hand the male-led sexism of mainstream politics. At certain times they were ignored and at others verbal assaults were common (Fearon, 1999). Despite being made unwelcome, the NIWC were able to act as mediators and conduits for information to parties that had been excluded from parts of the negotiation process. Peter Robinson, a future First Minister and leader of the DUP, declared that 'they (the NIWC) haven't been at the forefront of the battle when shots were being fired or when the constitution of Northern Ireland was in peril' (Peter Robinson quoted in Fearon, 1999: 14). In this instance, political participation is predicated on having taken part in violent political action and directly connected with male violence. Accordingly, women were not 'legitimate' actors on this stage. Deputy Leader of the SDLP, Seamus Mallon, said, in relation to the NIWC, that the peace negotiations 'won't be about setting differences aside, this will be about facing differences that we have in this community, facing them full-frontal and dealing with those differences. What we must realise is that these negotiations which are going to take place are going to be very hard-nosed and they are going to be real' (quoted in Fearon, 1999: 17). There was an assumption that women's 'peaceful' nature will not equip them to take part in hard or real politics or that the process of transversal politics would not be welcome or useful in the Forum.

The influence of the NIWC is visible in the Agreement, the clauses emphasising the 'right of women to full and equal political participation' and 'the advancement of women's right to be involved in public life' were lobbied for by the party. Unfortunately, concrete mechanisms have not emerged to ensure these goals become reality. Importantly, the NIWC were the key party lobbying for the inclusion of victims within the Agreement and the creation of a Civic Forum, which was intended to be a mechanism for civil society in Northern Ireland to have a voice in formal political matters, but which has fallen by the wayside due to a lack of political will (Pierson, 2018b).

The story of the NIWC has been extremely well documented and analysed as an example of women's organising and impact on peace negotiations (see for example Fearon, 1999; Murtagh, 2008). The creation of an all-women's party with a non-hierarchical structure based on the principles of inclusion, equality and human rights was a radical departure from the traditional zero-sum game politics of Northern Ireland. With the constitutional question being largely synonymous with politics in the region the NIWC were often dismissed as ineffectual or lacking in serious political clout whilst Fearon (1999) argues that many of their policies were co-opted by other parties indicating a wider reach than was perhaps recognised at the time. Murtagh (2008) argues that the NIWC brought community-based politics into the formal political realm and their lack of interest in 'winning' and focus on getting gender policy issues onto the agenda was confusing to their political opponents. After the Agreement the party's vote share fell considerably and after winning no seats in the 2006 election the party voluntarily disbanded. To describe this as a failure however is too simplistic an interpretation of the purpose and impact of the NIWC.

Since the Agreement, there have been a raft of subsequent agreements and community relations policies negotiating a range of political issues which are viewed to be tied to conflict. Many of these make brief reference to women in public life or women as builders of community however none make reference to any concrete measures to ensure women's participation in political life or in community peacebuilding. How the tokenistic reference to women in agreements has tangible outcomes for inclusion can be seen through the example of the case in the case of Re White (2000).[1] This case concerned a woman, Eileen White, who took a judicial review of appointments to the Parades Commission (the body tasked with mediating disputes on public processions), arguing that the failure to appoint any female members was discriminatory. The judge, Carswell LCJ, ruled that the Secretary of State had discretion to appoint an exclusively male membership to a significant public body (the Parades Commission), and that gender was not relevant to the issues with which the Parades Commission would be concerned. Rewriting this judgment from a feminist perspective, Catherine O'Rourke (2017) highlights the failure to consider women's participation in parades but also the effect of parades on women's lives. Gender in the original judgment is divorced from ethno-national identity, the lack of intersectionality allowing men to continue to speak, and make decisions, on behalf of women in their communities and to consider community in such a narrow way as to invisibilise gendered ethno-national identities and experiences.

Limited approaches to gender and women's inclusion have continued in subsequent peace talks and processes. The Commission on Flags, Identity, Culture and Tradition (FICT) which was established in June 2016 as part of the Fresh Start Agreement, to help the parties reach consensus on contentious issues surrounding flags, emblems and identity in Northern Ireland, and produce recommendations for the Executive (the administrative branch of the NI Assembly, made up of the First and Deputy First Ministers and eight departmental Ministers) to take forward was made up of fifteen members, only one of whom was a woman. Talks held in Cardiff in the summer of 2013 to reflect and consider contentious issues such as the policing of parades and display of flags, had three women out of more than thirty participants composed of police, politicians and community representatives (Pierson, 2019). US diplomat Richard Haass and Harvard Professor Meghan O'Sullivan were invited in 2013 to chair talks relating to parades and protests; flags, symbols and emblems; and contending with the past. The women's sector again observed women were generally excluded; however, Meghan O'Sullivan organised one meeting with women's groups.

Although there may be vague commitments to including women in talks and decision-making, when it comes to 'hard' political issues of peacebuilding and security male voices continue to be disproportionately represented in decision-making spheres and an approach which views gender as a wholly separate identity from ethno-national identity enables the exclusion of women's experiences within their communities from influencing policy and agreements.

The new and reformed institutions created from the Agreement were viewed to be legitimised through community involvement, who is viewed to represent a community becomes vitally important in who has the power to be heard in decision-making and by decision makers. The concept of community has been critiqued for its potential to homogenise its members. There is also the potential that those who dissent from community views may find their positions being dismissed or ignored as unrepresentative. As such, if a gendered or women-centered approach does not fit community narratives it may be pitted against the community and therefore presented as illegitimate. There is much work to be done, but much to be gained from approaching 'communities' as heterogeneous and with views that are constructed and contested over time rather than fixed and static.

Gender and political institutions

The formal political realm in Northern Ireland is largely typified through its continual cycle of crisis, whether that be conflict, political instability following the Agreement or more recently the outworking's of the UK leaving the European Union or larger global instabilities such as the COVID-19 pandemic. In the period since 1998 there have been five suspensions of the Northern Ireland (NI) Assembly lasting from one day to four years and, as Deiana et al. (2022) rightly notes, the constant level of crisis can work to marginalise other issues such as gender and sexuality, or view them as unimportant in the broader political landscape. However, it must also be considered that institutions are set up in ways that marginalise gender concerns and make it difficult to foreground them on the political agenda. The devolution of power to the NI Assembly and the use of consociational power-sharing have specific gendered effects on how political agendas are structured and decisions made. In order to interrogate political spaces and how change can come about it is first necessary to understand how spaces are gendered in their very design.

How women and gendered policy issues are included in political space is in part determined by how institutions are designed and function in practice. Institutions shape, and are shaped by, the political, economic and social forces within which they are embedded (MacKay, Kenny and Chappell 2010), therefore paying attention to the ways in which they are gendered will help us to understand the constraints and shapes political activity takes. Institutions can be gendered and gendering and can produce and reproduce unequal gender power relations. Gender relations play out in different ways, be that in the design of institutions or in the day-to-day interactions of those who work in them. Feminist institutionalism highlights that informal aspects of institutional life can be as important as formal practices in shaping how the institution function (Lowndes, 2020). This section will focus on two aspects which shape the operation of the Northern Ireland Assembly, its role as a devolved legislature and its power-sharing design.

Devolution of power is generally presented as a positive development for women. This is largely in reference to the descriptive and substantive representation of women and the potential for new political arenas to shed the traditional masculinity of older institutions (Mackay and McAllister, 2012). For example, academic work on Scotland and Wales points to a less adversarial form of politics and the pursuance of woman-friendly policies (Mackay and McAllister, 2012). Northern Ireland has not been presented in this same light. Research on devolved Assemblies in the UK has noted the particularly male-dominated and intimidating space of the Northern Ireland Assembly for women, and the distinct challenge for women to find their voice in such spaces (Shaw, 2013). Female politicians have voiced their own concerns about sexism and misogyny in the Assembly (Catriona Ruane, MLA and Megan Fearon, MLA quoted in Ashe, 2019b). Thomson (2016) outlines how the Assembly may suffer from 'nested newness', the idea that institutions cannot be blank slates and are informed by their institutional legacy. The Assembly cannot simply go from an institution that had historically low representation of women and a highly masculinised and sectarian form of politics to a woman-friendly arena without significant institutional and cultural transformation, such transformations take time and the embedding of women as political actors.

In terms of institutional legacy, Northern Irish politics before the Agreement suffered from very low representation of women coupled with what has been described as a 'martial' form of politics (Wilford, 1996). Prior to the Agreement only three women from Northern Ireland had been elected to Westminster (Wilford, 1996). Locally, representation of women has been low. Between 1921 and 1969 only nine women were elected to the Assembly, and in the interim periods of devolution in the 1970s and 1980s, only four women were elected in each time period. The highest level of female representation at council level never surpassed 15 per cent (Wilford, 1996). Politics and the creation of political parties was based on a militarised notion of protecting and defending the Union (for Unionists) and challenging and ending this Union (for Nationalists). Coupled with the political violence of the Troubles, the political arena was not viewed as a suitable arena for women. In many ways this assumption still exists, I have previously (Pierson, 2019) pointed to the low representation of women in talks about policing, community relations and legacy issues as continuance of delegitimising women's voices in politics.

The current design of governance is power-sharing. Consociationalism has become the model of choice in institutional design for societies emerging from violent conflict. The model, conceptualised by Lijphart in 1969, provides for the democratic management of divided communities based on the accommodation of politically salient communal identities within a power-sharing political system. It comprises four components: a grand coalition government, group autonomy in particular policy areas, proportional representation and a mutual group veto (Lijphart, 1977). Within 'corporate consociation' accommodated groups are pre-defined whereas in 'liberal consociation' the groups are self-defined and therefore can change over time (Lijphart, 1991). Northern Ireland represents a more liberal form of power-sharing where power-sharing partners are determined by the electorate and MLAs designate on entering the Assembly.

Byrne and McCulloch (2012) point to the gender paradox of power-sharing, in their analysis there is no inherent reason why women should not be able to reach equal inclusion under liberal power-sharing, yet experience and evidence suggest negative outcomes for women's descriptive and substantive political representation. However, some research has pointed to more positive outcomes, for example Bell's (2015) research which found that political settlements which adopted power-sharing were often coupled with gender quotas for elections. Feminist research and analysis on power-sharing both internationally and in the Northern Ireland context points to a negative relationship between gender and power-sharing based the fact that ethno-national identity is deemed to be the most politically salient identity and therefore marginalises and subordinates other identities including gender (Kennedy et al., 2016). This hegemony of ethnicity can also act to sectarianise issues to make them politically salient, for example, politicians stated that abortion (before decriminalisation) was an issue which united all political communities in their opposition to liberal laws (Pierson and Bloomer, 2017). Consociationalism has also been viewed to entrench ethno-national identity within divided societies and therefore the conservative gender roles that come with it. Power-sharing is conceived of as a tool of conflict management and stability rather than a process to transform conflict and identities; therefore, it can be positioned as at odds with feminist goals of destabilising gender hierarchies and identities (Deiana, 2013).

Feminist researchers often caution against the assumption that a presence of women will change processes or institutions to ensure better gender outcomes. However, documenting the presence of women within the new institutions helps to give a sense of the inroads that women have been able to make into the formal political realm. The Assembly has been slower than the other devolved Assemblies to increase women's descriptive representation, but representation has vastly increased. In 1998, the percentage of women in the Assembly stood at 13 per cent, by 2019 this had risen to 32 per cent (Uberoi et al., 2021). Women have also led four of Northern Ireland's political parties (the DUP, Sinn Féin, the Alliance Party and the Green Party). However, with an increase in women in leadership of political parties and in the Assembly a more progressive focus on gender policy issues cannot be assumed. Women cannot be assumed to automatically represent women or more liberal policy positions. On the topic of sexuality, openly homophobic statements have been made by female politicians, for example DUP MLA Iris Robinson in 2008 made comments both on local radio and in a Commons debate which stated that homosexuality was worse than child abuse (reported in Ashe, 2009). It was only in 2022, when Mal O'Hara was elected leader of the Green Party, that the first leader of a political party in Northern Ireland was openly gay.

In 2018, O'Hara hosted an Alternative Queer Ulster event at Parliament Buildings, this event being designed to bring alternative voices and experiences into formal political space, similar to Alternative Ms Ulster hosted by former Green Party leader Clare Bailey. On International Women's Day 2014 (8 March) Stormont (the Northern Ireland Assembly buildings) hosted the event titled Alternative Ms Ulster in response to the proposed staging of a beauty pageant, Miss Ulster, at Stormont the previous year. The event was intended to highlight the gender imbalance in public life through facilitating a range of women to speak in the Great Hall about what they believed needs to happen for Northern Ireland to become a better place for women to live. Media reports of the event after however fixated on the (false) notion that a woman (Cara Park) had appeared topless, with the Belfast Telegraph reporting 'Anger as topless woman speaks at Stormont' (Sweeney, 2014), selecting a range of quotes from male MLAs (who had not attended the event) commenting on the inappropriate behaviour. The media focus meant that the speeches made by twenty-five women on abortion, welfare cuts, political representation, sexism and gender-based violence were overshadowed by a morally conservative and sensationalist focus on one woman's body rather than her words. Political space is reserved for those who present themselves in a 'respectable' way, highlighting that women's behaviour in political space will be seen as more important than the issues they are advocating for.

Even those women who conform to conservative gendered attitudes and behaviour can still be reminded that their primary roles are in the private sphere. In 2016, when Arlene Foster became the first female leader of the DUP, Edwin Poots, a fellow DUP MLA, reminded her in the Assembly that her most important role continued to be as a wife, mother and daughter. Poots denied this was a sexist comment, stating that he was simply aware that Foster puts family above her political career. This of course ignores the fact that a comment like this has never been made to a male political leader, reminding him of his primary role as a husband, father and son. Comments such as this are reminiscent of early debates in the Assembly on abortion. These debates focused heavily on women's reasons for having abortions framed through a misogynistic understanding of abortion as a means to delay motherhood and selfishly prioritise careers and personal lives (Pierson and Bloomer, 2018). Such a presentation of abortion ignored the reality of abortion seekers (English department of health statistics illustrate that many of those seeking abortion from Northern Ireland were already mothers) yet serves to separate women into those who respect and prioritise conservative gender roles and stigmatise those who are perceived to not do so.

Outside of the NI Assembly, representation at local and national level has slightly increased. Women have been underrepresented at council level, with a modest increases from 14 per cent in 1997 to 25 per cent in 2014 (Gilmartin, 2021). In terms of Westminster elections, in 2019 22 per cent of those elected were women, this is substantively lower than the UK average of 29 per cent, however, it is a substantial increase from 11 per cent in 2015 (Galligan, 2020). There have been concerns raised about the lack of women in politics in Northern Ireland by international human rights bodies and by NI Assembly research. An Assembly and Executive Review Committee (2015) inquiry into women in politics identified many of the structural and institutional barriers that women face worldwide. Issues such as confidence, institutional misogyny, treatment by the media, childcare and adversarial culture of politics were all highlighted within the report. The committee made a range of recommendations for parties such as party membership strategies, mentoring, diversity training and maternity and paternity leave policies and strategies for the Assembly such as public engagement, a working group on gender sensitivity and the creation of a women's caucus (NI Assembly, 2015). Interestingly, the committee could not come to a conclusive decision on quotas, a concrete measure which would ensure parity of representation on gender.

Women's participation in politics does not necessarily mean a more feminist politics. Niall Gilmartin's (2018) research with Republican women who were active as combatants, and their experiences after conflict, decouples women in electoral politics from feminism. Whilst Republican women are a very visible part of the formal political terrain, Gilmartin points to a lessening of a radical feminist influence on Republican politics. The research participants attributed this to the change in political organising and a shift in political space 'from the streets to Stormont'. The movement of Republican politics away from non-hierarchical community organizing towards a top-down institutionalised approach encourages a narrowly liberal understanding of feminism and as such many of the women involved in Gilmartin's research have become disillusioned with formal politics, preferring to organise in community settings. Thus, whilst Republicanism can point to a higher number of women in political leadership positions it does not necessarily follow that this furthers a feminist political project.

In terms of support for, and trust in, political institutions there is evidence of a gender divide. Hayes and McAllister (2013) found men to be consistently more supportive than women in their views and trust of institutions and lower levels of support from Protestant women than their Catholic counterparts (51 per cent and 54 per cent respectively). More recent research on public opinions on power-sharing also indicates a clear gendered dimension to political participation in Northern Ireland. Women are less likely than men to express their political opinions online (9 per cent and 21 per cent respectively); less likely to contact their MLA (10 per cent and 18 per cent respectively); less likely to watch the proceedings of the Assembly (25 per cent and 34 per cent respectively); and less likely to attend a political meeting (1 per cent and 7 per cent respectively) (Haughey and Loughran, 2021: 18). Whilst there is an increase in women within political institutions, there is still work to do in ensuring that women feel represented and included by, and trust in, political institutions.

However, politicians do believe that they are acting on behalf of women's interests. Haughey (2023) surveyed MLAs who indicated, across the political spectrum, that they acted on behalf of women's organisations (an overall score of 5.5 was found, where 7 indicated 'great importance', with no significant difference based on party affiliation). There is evidence to suggest that some critical actors are pushing forward issues of gender equality, this can be illustrated in the form of Private Members Bills. In 2022, the Period Products Bill was proposed by SDLP MLA Pat Catney. The bill places a duty on the Department for Communities to make period products available to those who need them. In 2022, the Department of Education confirmed funding of more than £400,000 to provide free period products to schools. In 2023, the Abortion Services (Safe Access Zones) Act was passed. Introduced by Clare Bailey of the Green Party, it protects the right of women to access abortion and associated sexual and reproductive health services through the creation of buffer zones outside of health service locations. The Domestic Abuse and Civil Proceedings Act 2021 was introduced by Naomi Long of the Alliance Party and criminalises abusive behaviour that occurs on two or more occasions against an intimate partner, former partner or close family member.

Conclusion

This chapter has attempted to illustrate the social and political constructions of identity in Northern Ireland, in particular the interplay of gender and ethno-national identity and its role in constraining and shaping women's political opportunities and participation. The chapter illustrates how particularly conservative constructions of gender identity formulate certain roles for men and women, which they do not necessarily have to follow, but may find it difficult to break free from. These roles have strong implications for how women negotiate political spaces and how they are heard when in these spaces. In particular, the equation of women with conciliation and peace may in fact constrain work around broader political questions, continuing to position women outside of debates on the future of Northern Ireland, peacebuilding and security issues.

Political institutions are also gendered structures and as illustrated above are set up in ways which prioritise particular identities over others. This hegemony of ethno-national identity means that even when women are in political spaces their demands must be framed within the dominant framework of ethno-nationalism to make it onto the political agenda. Gender concerns have been minimised in political agreements since the Agreement onwards and the invisibility of gender as a political identity and political concern frames the environment within which feminist actors work. This chapter has examined the political structures and identities which shape political activity in Northern Ireland, the following chapters interrogate how feminists build a movement and negotiate with these political structures to advance gender equality.

Note

1 White R V Court of Appeal in Northern Ireland, 2 November 2000. https://www.casemine.com/judgement/uk/5a8ff8d560d03e7f57ecdfd8 (last accessed 12/02/2025).

2

Feminist movement building and collective identity

Feminist political movements are comprised of a broad array of actors working towards a range of visions of gender equality or freedom. Any attempt to provide a definitive account of feminist political activity or space will undoubtably fail to cover every group or actor. As documented in the previous chapter, there is a strong culture and history of organising on gendered political issues and for feminist goals in Northern Ireland (NI). However, the complexity of politics and the dominance of the conflict narrative means that other strands of political activity can be invisible or deemed of secondary importance. One factor which has made NI feminism more prominent internationally is the abortion rights movement and its success in decriminalising abortion in 2019, but this is only one strand of the ongoing feminist movement building and its collective action. The aim of this chapter is to contextualise and situate contemporary feminist organising and movement building both as counterparts to the broader politics of Northern Ireland and within global contemporary feminist movements. In this way, it paints a picture of how feminism has claimed space in the politics of contemporary Northern Ireland creating a powerful *subaltern counterpublic* (Fraser, 1999) from which to advocate collectively for women's rights. Whilst later chapters will look at the strategies and discourses used by feminist actors this chapter focuses on how a movement has been built and the continuing challenges in feminist movement building.

Feminist movement building has challenged conventions from wider social movements which are often rooted in masculine assumptions about what issues and activities count as legitimate forms of activism (Wulff et al., 2015). For example, issues such as reproductive health and gender-based violence have previously been considered part of the private sphere and therefore depoliticised and ignored as inequalities. Feminist groups also work to challenge gender relations and gender identities, going beyond movement work focused on the state and economy into culture and collective and individual identity. Feminist organising often challenges ideas of leadership, attempting to flatten hierarchies and facilitate collective consensus building.

In this way, interrogating feminist movement building has much to teach wider social and political movements.

However, contemporary feminist movements are not without challenges and a number of ongoing tensions exist. In contemporary feminist organising in the Global North, understandings around gender definitions and exclusionary ideas of who counts as a woman have created environments which are harmful to trans women. Whilst those who identify as trans-exclusionary feminists comprise a small part of the movement, the focus on these ideas in wider cultural and political discourse implies a certain dominance in movements. Intersectionality, whilst dominant in the language of organising, still remains difficult in practice and in particular the dominance of white and middle-class voices in feminist groups is an ongoing challenge. This chapter will situate Northern Ireland within these contemporary debates, examining the dynamics and ongoing challenges in building a common political agenda and feminist voice.

Movement building and collective identity

Social movements are considered an important part of the democratic process in their role as challengers to the state and their use of unconventional political participation (Della-Porta, 2020). They have been defined as transgressive and disruptive, attempting to gain the attention of the public and political decision makers, making use of a range of activities and strategies to make collective claims. They are considered informal networks of individuals, groups and organisations engaged in action on the basis of a shared collective identity. Collective identities involve defining movement goals, means of achieving goals and finding a common language and voice. This shared collective identity is what sustains movements in terms of cohesion and commitment enabling the building of political spaces around a shared identity and goals (Flesher-Fominaya, 2010). However, Saunders (2008) cautions that we cannot expect movements to have a singular collective identity and should pay attention to group identities and dynamics which make up movements as a whole.

Collective identity building is recognised as a dynamic process, shaped by interactions between individuals building 'the shared definition of a group that derives from members' common interests, experiences and solidarity' (Taylor and Whittier, 1992: 105). Meluccis work on the collective identities of new social movements in the European context argues that collective identity replaces class consciousness as a factor in attachment and mobilisation in movements (Melucci, 1995; Hunt and Benford, 2004). Collective identity does not mean that actors do not necessarily have to be in complete agreement on ideologies, beliefs, interests or goals in order to come together and generate collective action (Flesher-Fominaya, 2010: 399) but that there is an ability to distinguish what makes 'us' and that we can be recognised by others. Social movement actors should also be able to build and recognise their identity in relation to the broader social and political context and build awareness of how this shapes opportunities and constraints in movement action.

Collective identities are built on a process of boundary work, the process of defining who 'we' are involves defining who 'we are not'. This process can be engaged with within movements, for example, in feminist movements this has taken place in the past on positions on pornography and sex work or on the utility of engaging with state institutions such as the police. The process can also take place between movements and of course between dominant political and social groups. However, there are often cross-cutting ties between social movements with actors moving across groups, enabling the potential for coalitions between groups and less likelihood of incompatible identities. Boundary work can also act as a process of exclusion. For those who have not been part of the process of defining collective identity or who may not speak the common language of the group this may act as a barrier to participation. Collective identities can shift and change over time and, as they can be intimately linked with individual member's identities and experiences (this is particularly common in women's movements), there will be continual negotiation and redefinition as members change. As identities are forged through daily interaction, it is common for strong collective identities to emerge when movements are in a period of high activity and for this to sustain movements during periods of abeyance.

Feminist movements and collective identity

Feminist mobilization is manifest both in territorially delimited movements and in multiple transnational movements that connect across borders in global processes (Weldon et al., 2023: 1). In this way, defining a collective identity and voice for feminism involves interrogating national movements within global trends. Feminism is also not a monolithic ideology, and it is more accurate to talk of feminisms, with differing positions on core issues dependent on differing ideological strands, personal perspectives and experiences. Previous work on feminist and women's movements has highlighted that identity formation is not a static process and that feminists are often able to talk across differences. As with the critique of transversal dialogue between women's movements in divided societies (explored in the previous chapter), we must interrogate to what extent talking across differences happens and how it helps movements deal with difficult issues.

One method for contextualising the positions and identities of differing feminist movements has been through the umbrella of the waves metaphor. The idea of feminism coming in waves is a useful metaphor to encompass the idea of periods of intense activity followed by periods of abeyance whilst all remaining part of a trajectory of continuing activity. More recent characterisations have described this continuance of feminist organising as a river, allowing for more continuance of activity and blending of ideology and people within the metaphor, in which 'there are rapids, sometimes it is very shallow or deep, sometimes there are rocks or other obstacles that divert its course, sometimes it is wide, at other times narrow, sometimes it overflows at the banks, sometimes there is a drought' (Crossley, 2017: 20). Positioning feminism within the broader waves metaphor helps to identify common organising features and common identities from which to examine feminism in Northern Ireland.

Defining which wave we are currently working within is difficult. First wave (correlated with the suffrage movement) and second wave (associated with feminism in the 1960s and 1970s, which brought private sphere issues such as abortion and gender-based violence into public political consciousness) are usually defined as distinct periods of activity whereas third and fourth wave feminism are harder to define both in terms of chronology and what issues are the focal point of the movement. Previous waves of feminism are considered to have more distinct collective identities, with the first wave associated with civil and political rights and the second with the politicisation of private sphere concerns and the idea of a global sisterhood (the nostalgia of collective identity has been challenged in particular by Black feminism). Dean (2009) has called the wave metaphor an empty signifier in particular with regard to third-wave feminism, yet this can be interpreted as a positive development, attempting to move away from a monolithic view of what feminism is or entails. Evans (2014) contends that the wave metaphor can be viewed as chronological but also can be viewed as generational (feminists may identify as being part of different waves in the same time period), ideological (when particular strands of feminist thought, radical, liberal, socialist, post-structuralist become identified with a particular set of activities) or oppositional (when new groups of feminists specifically distance themselves from what has gone before).

As noted, defining what third- and fourth wave feminism is remains difficult and in fact defining whether there is a distinct third and fourth wave is part of this problem. Third-wave feminism has been described as a feminist commitment to intersectional inclusion and social justice issues yet conversely identified as part of a neoliberal individualist agenda (Evans,

2014; Fraser, 2013). The third wave is also identified with developing poststructuralist thought in the 1990s, specifically the work of Judith Butler, who challenged binary and fixed understandings of gender identity and the term 'woman'. The fourth wave of feminism has been distinguished from previous waves often on the basis of the move to online activism (Munro, 2013) which has enabled the emergence of online feminist communities and global attention and voice on issues such as gender-based violence and transnational flow of solidarity and strategy. The fourth wave has also seen a recommitment to intersectionality and the breakdown of strict gender categories and binaries. Early accounts of a fourth wave in the US context have linked it to a reaction to violence and extremism experienced by women in the post-9/11 global war on terror and a need to 'confront a new and devastating reality' in the form of increasing imperialism and global capitalism (Kaplan, 2003: 55). Of course, how 'new' this was for women in global majority countries is debatable, emphasising the fact that waves are not a truly global metaphor.

Invoking the wave metaphor can be contentious. Feminist theorists have pointed out that conceptualising feminist movements in waves focuses predominantly on the Global North, ignoring differing trajectories of feminist thought and activism globally. Within the Global North it can marginalise the work of women of colour, LGBT+ feminists and class differences within feminist organising. It also has the effects of invoking a linear progression of women's rights and creating an oppositional stance between different waves. Evans and Chamberlain (2015) provide a thoughtful approach to feminist movements and waves. They argue that a more fluid and reflective deployment of the term can encourage us to think about continuities between waves and how they interact and intersect, multiplicity of thought and action when multiple waves coexist and inclusivity. This is useful for examining collective identities and mobilisations as waves help to think through generational differences and how identities develop in contexts where goals of previous waves (abortion rights) have only recently been achieved.

All movements are situated within their own institutional, political, cultural and social contexts, however, situating Northern Ireland within global wave narratives presents some problems. Conflict and the dominance of ethno-national and constitutional politics have been posited as a reason why a strong second and third wave of feminism was less distinct or developed in the region, and the fact that second-wave goals, such as abortion rights, continued to be fought for until recently troubles the wave narrative. Graff's work in the Polish context (noted in the introduction to this book), highlights how certain contexts can be difficult to situate within the wave metaphor or can be viewed by those outside to 'have missed the feminist boat'

(2003: 101). This difficulty of situating feminism in Northern Ireland can be viewed within mainstream literature on contemporary feminist organising. In writing which considers the UK context, Northern Ireland is generally absent from texts (see for example Evans, 2014; Dean, 2012; MacKay, 2008). Within texts on the Irish women's movement, there is often a chapter on Northern Ireland but as an outlier, it continues to sit as a place apart from the wider context (Connolly and O'Toole, 2005). When Northern Ireland is written about in gendered terms it is often with regard to the intersection and effects between gender and conflict. I do not mention this to present it as a negative, a strong unique movement reflective of organising in distinct circumstances and around specific concerns is incredibly valuable, but to point out that this organising has been invisible within wider feminist discourses.

Establishing a collective identity within feminism involves organising under the banner of 'women' or 'feminism' and making political decisions about inclusion, strategy and a common political agenda or ways to formulate political demands. This chapter will examine how movement building has developed in Northern Ireland through its development of networks and coalitions, its negotiation of inclusion, identity and intersectionality, generational divides and ongoing tensions and challenges. In this way, the chapter examines both the building of a contemporary movement and how it can be situated within contemporary global movements and ongoing feminist waves. First, we turn to a brief history of feminist organising in NI.

Feminist organising in Northern Ireland

In order to examine contemporary feminist organising and the processes to create a collective voice and vision it is necessary to outline the landscape of feminist groups both historically and contemporarily. This cannot be an exhaustive list of groups and organisations but will outline core groups and the key issues for activist groups. I am conceptualising activism separately from the more formalised women's and community sector and including those groups which are more explicitly activist in their orientation. They are perhaps more diffuse in their organisation and hierarchy, and are often not located in formal premises or with distinct constitutions and/or paid employees. Of course, as a small society, many of those who work in the women's sector are often involved in feminist activist groups and many of these groups work and overlap with the more formalised women's sector.

As Carmel Roulston writes of second-wave feminism in Northern Ireland, many of those who would have been involved in feminist movement building elsewhere had their energies diverted by the civil rights movement (1989). Organisations such as the Campaign for Social Justice and the Northern

Ireland Civil Rights Association had many women members campaigning against discrimination in employment, biased allocation of housing and an undemocratic electoral system (Cockburn, 2013). Tara Keenan-Thomson has illustrated the emergence of women into the civil rights movement in the early 1960s, primarily through protests at the discriminatory allocation of public housing, yet notes that in contrast to dominant theories exploring women in social protest these women 'failed to develop a new political consciousness regarding their place within the gender regime' (Keenan-Thomson, 2010: 96). In fact, stereotypical notions of gender roles were often used (particularly in housing protests) to emphasise the respectability of such protests. Monica McWilliams notes the more conservative attitude towards women's participation in the public sphere via employment statistics. By 1971 only 29 per cent of married women were economically active in Northern Ireland compared to 42 per cent in Britain (McWilliams, 2002). As such, although some women in Northern Ireland were active in questioning discriminatory behaviour on ethno-national grounds they were less likely to question traditional domestic roles.

Many women went on to become active in civil rights campaigns and although their work often challenged the gender regime, some were reluctant to engage with feminism. For example, Betty Sinclair, a key activist in the Communist Party of Northern Ireland, became the 'Chairman' of the Northern Ireland Civil Rights Association (NICRA); however, her ideological positioning did not allow her to acknowledge the significance of her gender as a leader. She explained that being a woman meant little to her and that 'feminism is not a working-class outlook' (Betty Sinclair quoted in Keenan-Thomson, 2010: 142). Patricia McCluskey, leader of the Campaign for Social Justice, used conservative gender roles to explain women's lack of interest in the broader civil rights movement as it encompassed aspects of public life such as employment, which may be of more interest to men.

The connection to civil rights groups and material conditions of social and economic inequality has been credited with giving Northern Irish feminism more working-class representation than other feminist movements of the time. The early 1970s saw the burgeoning of explicitly feminist movements with groups forming in Belfast's Ormeau Road and in universities. These groups focussed on issues such as childcare and gender-based violence. The Northern Ireland Women's Rights Movement was set up in 1975 emerging from Queen's University Women's Liberation Group in 1973 and was connected to the Northern Ireland Civil Rights Association, trade union members and members of the Communist Party of Ireland. The mobilisation of this group into a federation of groups across Northern Ireland and particularly engaging working-class women was ultimately unsuccessful. Women's movements, of course, split all over the world and the NIWRM had similar disagreements over male members with a split for some into a Socialist Women's Group. NIWRM decided not to take a position over the constitutional question but did condemn violence from both the state and paramilitary groups. The SWG, which then became the Belfast Women's Collective, was critical of this 'non-position'. Many of the women involved in feminist activism during this period went on to form the Northern Ireland Women's Coalition.

The NIWRM opened Northern Ireland's first women's centre in Belfast city centre in 1979. The Downtown Women's Centre was a meeting space for activists in organisations such as the Northern Ireland Abortion Campaign and the Belfast Women's Collective (Hill, Walker, and Ward, 2018 cited in O'Keeffe, 2021). The Downtown Women's Centre has been credited as a space where contentious issues were debated and interrogated, their 'Women into Politics' project encouraged confrontation with sectarianism and political differences and encouraged women's representation in politics (regardless of which political party member they were affiliated with) has been noted as an important aspect of women's organising around the time of the peace process (Porter, 2000).

More recent feminist activism can be broadly situated within the literature considering the third and/or fourth wave of feminism as outlined above. As Aune and Redfern (2010: 10) writes 'since the start of the millennium, a staggering number of feminist organisations and campaigning groups have formed...' Some of the longest-established contemporary activist groups bridge the wave distinction in time periods, this includes abortion rights groups Alliance for Choice Belfast and Alliance for Choice Derry. Until relatively recently abortion rights groups were largely acting on their own with many women's, community and human rights groups stating neutral positions on abortion (Pierson and Bloomer, 2017). Alliance for Choice Belfast was set up in 1996 to campaign for the extension of the 1967 Abortion Act to Northern Ireland and the Alliance for Choice Derry grew out of the Women's Right to Choose Group which started in the 1980s (O'Brien, 2022). Both groups have been involved in helping women access abortion through the provision of abortion pills and facilitating travel abroad, lobbying successive governments first to extend the 1967 Act and then to decriminalise and provide a broad range of educational, social and cultural activities aimed at changing conversations and mindsets on abortion. The Alliance for Choice Derry moved away from direct political action of lobbying politicians and responding to consultations on abortion in favour of community education and awareness raising after defeats in extending the 1967 Abortion Act to Northern Ireland under the Labour government in 2000, and again in 2008 (Drapeau-Bisson, 2020). Since the decriminalisation of abortion in 2019, abortion activism has not ended both because of the lack of service provision and because there is a continued need to challenge stigmatising views on abortion (see Chapter 5 for more detail on abortion provision beyond decriminalisation).

More recent groups, which fit within the more recent rise of feminist groups, include the Belfast Feminist Network and Reclaim the Agenda which were both set up in 2010. The Belfast Feminist Network (BFN) is an informal collection of diverse voices and positions on feminist issues with an online presence on Facebook and Twitter. BFN has organised informal talks, debates and seminars and participated in protests and activist training days. Deiana (2013) writes of their campaign to raise awareness around sexual assault which culminated in a short film, a piece of research on perceptions of sexual violence and an event engaging with the public and key bodies such as politicians, the police and Women's Aid. BFN has also worked on the gendered impacts of austerity and changes to welfare policy engaging with trade unions and the women's sector. An attempt to remain non-hierarchical in organisation sees a diffuse identity for the group and in more recent years more of an online than physical presence; however, the BFN was able to co-ordinate protests and demonstrations outside Belfast Crown Court at the time of what was called the Ulster rugby rape trial.[1]

Reclaim the Agenda was explicitly formed in reaction to cuts to funding of women's centres and is made up of feminist activists, women's sector representatives and trade unionists. Its key themes are very much focussed on the material inequalities in women's lives including poverty, discrimination, healthcare, gender-based violence, representation and childcare.[2] The group has also been a central focal point for organising International Women's Day (IWD) themes, activities and marches such as Reclaim the Night marches which have been happening annually since 2014. Much of this work has value in reclaiming women's history and making this visible in the public sphere through the use of renaming streets after women, undertaking HERitage bus tours and a mural commemorating women's history and suffrage on the Shankill Road. Reclaiming history has also involved engaging with difficult and sometimes divisive histories, for example, the 2016 IWD programme was 'Reclaim the 2016 Agenda' which recognised that the events of the 1916 Easter Rising[3] centenary in Ireland would be co-opted by particular groups and could largely be divisive. However, to not confront this past leaves women's histories as one-dimensional and hollow and in fact helps the work of disconnecting women from being actors in national struggles rather than helpers or bystanders.

As noted above, feminist movements collective voice is often characterised through the wave metaphor with distinct goals, ideals, issues and activities motivating successive waves. The waves are often perceived as generational shifts often with less consideration as to how they intersect and interact with each other. In Northern Ireland the activism depicted above, whilst taking place across time periods, often involves the same groups of people working across different waves of feminism including second, third and potentially fourth wave. In writing about feminism in NI, different interpretations of this inter-generational movement building have been taken. Cynthia Cockburn, revisiting Belfast in 2012, writes that the new generation of 'post-millennial' feminism is in direct contrast to previous generations of organising, with less of a focus on community and class politics (Cockburn, 2013). However, this observation fails to recognise the reach of such a broad-based coalition of women and may fall into what Dean (2010) describes as part of a left nostalgia where previous eras of feminist activism are harked back to as eras where there was less division and more of a common 'sisterhood', this nostalgia tends to erase the key sites of difference which arise in all movements, including feminism. This is particularly important in the NI context where, as noted, positions on the constitutional issue including neutrality have caused divisions within feminism.

The value of a broader range of groups working on a range of issues and utilising a variety of strategies has been shown to be full of potential. Maria Deiana argues that the instances of inter-generational feminist activism could play an important role in a concerted effort to enhance women's citizenship claims in the public sphere and readdress the gender shortcoming of Northern Ireland's incomplete peace (Deiana, 2013). Further to this, Kellie Turtle (2015) uses the example of Reclaim the Agenda and the Belfast Feminist Network to underscore the overlap in members and the support and learnings that a newer less structured organisation such as the BFN can take from an organisation with more experienced members and more links to state feminism and vice versa as groups that are more removed from state feminism can engage in more radical and cultural change work needed to shift gender conservatism and inequality.

Identity and feminist politics in the NI context

As this text has established, there is an overarching political structure in Northern Ireland which is male-dominated, often rooted in crisis and focused on ensuring conflict management through balancing relations and equality between the two dominant communities. In recent political attitudes surveys, there are increasing numbers of people who do not define themselves within these binary understandings of identity, with at least four out of every ten people in Northern Ireland describing themselves as 'Neither Unionist nor Nationalist' (Hayward and McManus, 2019). Interestingly, the largest group of people identifying as 'Neither' are women

(61 per cent of those identifying as 'Neither' in the 2017 Northern Ireland Life and Times Survey identify as female). Whilst women have always been involved in ethno-national politics and movements, it has been posited that they are more likely to reject male-dominated and patriarchal politics and have been shown to have less trust in political institutions (Hayes and McAllister, 2013). The rejection of binary labels of Unionist or Nationalist has been explained through the lens of political apathy, congruent with the experiences of other regions emerging from political and violent conflict (Hayward and McManus, 2019). Nevertheless, this should be defined as apathy with formal electoral politics rather than all political organising.

With this electoral political apathy comes a substantial proportion of non-voters, around half of those who identify as 'Neither' did not vote in the 2019 elections (Tonge, 2020). Those from this group who do vote are most likely to vote for the Alliance Party. However, as Tonge (2020) notes it is difficult to ascertain whether the Alliance Party is rejecting ethno-national binary identities or accommodating them within its structure. The contentious and crisis-driven nature of politics in the region may mean that those who do not wish to engage in sectarian politics may want to disengage from formal politics altogether. Whilst the Alliance and Green parties have seen rising numbers in the past ten years, it is also important that there are spaces to be political outside of the formal electoral political sphere as one participant explained:

> I suppose I was always very aware growing up about how everything is framed in a very, not even talking about Catholic or Protestant, but a very macho framework. People were listening to the people who were the loudest in the room. Not necessarily the people who were the most forward-thinking or sensible. Respect and community leadership actually came from fear…so I suppose in recognizing all that trying to find somewhere where you feel like there's a community that doesn't have to be given a big national identity label where people can feel safe.[4]

Feminist organising, as well as potentially operating outside the framework of sectarian politics, can also provide a space beyond the male-dominated patriarchal arena of formal and community politics. However, it would be naïve to assume that dominant political identities sit completely outside feminist politics. As outlined in the previous chapter, women's groups in Northern Ireland were described by Cynthia Cockburn in the 1990s as operating through the lens of transversal dialogue and politics. This approach of negotiating identity has been critiqued as ignoring or minimising differences between groups of women which may discourage some women from participating in feminist organising or women's groups.

Feminism as a movement is associated with, at a minimum, the achievement of equality and rights. In the Northern Ireland context, these terms have politicised understandings and have often been framed and perceived to be more readily taken on by those who identify as Nationalist or Republican. This perception has roots in the civil rights movement in Northern Ireland which highlighted inequalities against Catholic communities and the use of international and regional human rights mechanisms during conflict against abuses by state institutions, which were more heavily staffed by Protestant populations. Perceptions about rights and equality issues and their link to identity may leak into feminist spaces in different ways. In some cases, it may lead to replications of ethno-national balance when allocating speakers to events, as one participant noted with regards to her Protestant identity 'I do think it's the reason why sometimes I might be picked over somebody else to speak on a panel'.[5] However, the sense that Unionism and feminism are not compatible identities may be shared by some feminists, as the same participant explained 'I've been told by people that they've been told to dial back on their Unionism in feminist spaces because that automatically leads to, you know, accusations of colonialism or whatever else'.

The role of ethno-national identity in feminist spaces, and in particular, those who identify as Unionist or Loyalist is under-examined. Historically, Unionist and Loyalist women have been viewed to have a minimal role in politics with strict gender ideologies situating them as subservient to men both in the public and private sphere (Sales, 1997). This has been solidified through the lack of representation of Unionist women in electoral and community politics. More recent academic work has examined Loyalist women's involvement in protest (Ashe, 2006; Byrne, 2013), for example, the involvement of women in the Holy Cross dispute[6] of the early 2000s or the more recent flag protests at Belfast City Hall at the removal of the Union Flag.[7] However, this work examines these women as gendered ethno-national actors rather than feminist actors. A recent project which has specifically engaged Loyalist and feminist identity is the online site 'Her Loyal Voice', an online platform of blogs and interviews which aim to provide a safe space for Loyalist women to share their lived experiences. They define feminism within Loyalism as:

> We are part of the global feminist movement and by holding space as Loyalist Feminists we reject the notion that feminism is ideologically situated in the Republican movement. Loyalist Feminism aims to create an emancipatory knowledge and information base particular to the needs of and informed by the experiences of Loyalist women. Our oppression as women and gender and sexual minorities must be addressed within our own cultural context and the cultural context of Loyalist women is different from our mainstream feminist counterparts and middle-class Unionist women.[8]

This quote, whilst identifying a place for Loyalist women in feminism, clearly positions that place as counter to 'mainstream' movement building and in contrast to both Republicanism and Unionism. Many of the articles and interviews on their website talk about feminist issues such as reproductive rights and gender-based violence yet there is a strong thread of fear of a threat of cultural erosion. Some of their interviews are anonymous fearing both misogynistic and sectarian abuse indicating that there is backlash against these women both in their own communities and from other communities. The fact that much of this work has stayed online and is less visible in mainstream feminist spaces indicates there is still some way to go in accommodating wider political difference in feminist space.

The work of locating ethno-national identity within the feminist movement and its collective identity is vitally important. Political discussions regarding the future of Northern Ireland, whether that be as part of the UK or as part of a reunified Ireland, are gaining increased momentum. Having feminist voices in those conversations and the consideration of women's rights is necessary to avoid gender equality within any new structures becoming an afterthought. These conversations must also include a diverse range of women's voices and perspectives, not only those who may be seen to more naturally fit in feminist spaces.

Intersectionality

Intersectionality has been a feature of feminist organising, particularly in third and fourth wave feminism and specifically recognises inequality and oppression as a multi-layered experience and attempts to foster inclusion on this basis. Intersectional approaches to organising can be traced to the Combahee River Collective, a Black feminist lesbian socialist organization active in Boston in the United States in the mid- to late-1970s. Frustrated with mainstream second-wave feminist movements in the United States and their dominance by white women and sole focus on gender as the sole source of oppression, the Combahee River Collective statement laid down the foundations of their work and its aspirations. The foundations of this work are intersectional, as they state, 'We also often find it difficult to separate race from class from sex oppression because in our lives they are most often experienced simultaneously' (Combahee River Collective Statement, 1977: 504). In the 1980s, the term intersectionality was coined by lawyer Kimberle Crenshaw to explain the limitations of anti-discrimination laws which can recognise race or gender discrimination but not how these forms of discrimination overlap and intersect to create specific experiences of inequality. She argues that in the US context, African

American women and other women of colour are left with less recourse to justice.

Intersectionality has become a core feature of feminist organising since the 1990s. Paying attention to intersectionality within movement building can mean addressing power relations among members, it can be used as a means to assess the difficulties in developing coalitions between different groups of women, or the challenges in forming a political agenda. In its most formal sense, it can be used to assess diversity and inclusion within groups. Intersectionality is not easy to achieve, as Alison Phipps writes about the global #MeToo movement against sexual violence, this movement whilst started by a Black woman only achieved widespread media and global attention when famous white women began to speak out. As Phipps writes, this is more insidious, going beyond inclusion but that 'the cultural power of white tears, which underpins movements such as the viral iteration of #MeToo, is a racialised and classed power which relies on the illegibility of women of colour, and Black women especially, as victims' (Phipps, 2021: 92). Whiteness has political and cultural power which can invisibilise some women as legitimate victims of violence. Intersectionality must be deployed intentionally and with continuous reflection on power relations in a movement for it to have any chance of success.

In the British context, Evans writes that contemporary feminism has a less coherent understanding of intersectionality than US counterparts (Evans, 2016). Intersectionality has been blamed by those critical of contemporary feminist organising for a less collective approach to identity and a push-back against recognition of differential experiences of womanhood. Such critique is part of the wider hostile environment towards the inclusion of trans women within the feminist movement which dominates mainstream discussions about feminism in Britain currently (Pearce et al., 2020). This is not to say that there are no intersectional groups in Britain, for example, the work of the group Sisters Uncut on domestic violence throughout the UK is explicitly described as an 'intersectional feminist direct-action collective'. Evans (2016) work on feminist groups in universities also reveals a commitment to, and normalisation of, intersectionality as a concept. Student-led feminist groups often explicitly label themselves as intersectional and are keen to discuss the complexities and outworkings of this in their organising and movement building.

Intersectionality is a theory under construction (Cho et al., 2013), investigating its application in praxis helps us to analyse how it is understood in context, how it is used and how it is shaped and changed through use. Social context is very important, the historical, economic and political conditions within which we organise have consequences for how we recognise and act on inequality and oppression. Examining intersectionality in the case of Northern Ireland is particularly interesting as difference has always been part of the feminist experience, with overarching ethno-national identity always present and a recognition that there is a diversity of experience, and not always a common political identity, for women. As presented in the previous section, there is continuous reflection needed on how identity is negotiated. Class has also been noted as an important factor in NI feminism via the strong network of women's groups which often supplanted state service provision during the conflict. Identity has previously been discussed within the framing of transversal politics, as noted above, a rooting and shifting approach which does not ignore differing ethno-national positions but negotiates them when working on gender issues. Considering this through an intersectional lens, one participant found that this legacy meant that the inclusion of trans women within feminism is less contentious in Northern Ireland than in Britain:

> how we're responding to challenges is different, and I do think that's because we have to work across difference, you know, since some of his movement started. So I think there was space made for difference, and working together on uncommon goals, despite having different opinions on other things that then meant when other differences were introduced, so particularly thinking about trans women, that was just another different type of woman that you were organizing with.[9]

This is not to say that there is no transphobia within NI feminism, yet it was felt to be in the minority rather than the majority:

> So I know that there's one or two people around who hold views like that (transphobic views). But they're very much a minority, and there are people online. You cannot be sure where they're from. How many of you actually are using like five or six accounts to represent one person. Are they really here, or are they somewhere else? it's not as big a problem yet (as in Britain), but that doesn't mean to say it"s not a problem.[10]

A commitment to intersectional praxis was mentioned by everyone who took part in the interviews. This commitment was approached largely from the perspective of inclusion and attempting to diversify the range of people who take part in feminist organising. Race was noted to be an area within feminist organising where there was more work to do and more conversations to have, however, these conversations need to go further than talking about inclusion:

> We had a workshop where it was opening up the conversation around whiteness and how we need to be more inclusive but in a non-threatening way, that

if you didn't know what intersectionality is you were still welcome to be part of the of the conversation and I do think that maybe that's what we can continue doing – some activities or doing some other events so that more people are comfortable and join in the conversation.[11]

Race has largely been ignored in the politics of Northern Ireland. Racial equality legislation was only introduced in 1997, thirty years after the rest of the UK and was heavily resisted by both Unionist and Nationalist politicians on the basis that there was no racism in NI (Crangle, 2018). This period of neglect was disturbed by the advent of the peace process and the development of good relations policies enabling conversations about discrimination beyond ethno-national identity. The growth of an ethnic minority population has also come with the end of violent conflict, in 1995 only four to six thousand people identified as being from an ethnic minority background whereas the 2021 census shows 65,600 people or 3.4 per cent of the population. With the rise of an ethnic minority population came increased rates of hate crimes often against Roma, Chinese and more recently Muslim communities (Knox, 2011).

As Gilligan (2019) writes, policies and laws on racial equality are focused on achieving formal equality or punishing racial discrimination rather than challenging or eradicating racism. Within research on race in NI, there is almost no consideration of the intersection between race and gender and the specific experiences of women from ethnic minority populations in NI. MacNamara et al. (2020) consider the policy response to Female Genital Cutting (FGC) in the region through an intersectional feminist lens highlighting how a Global North gender framework, and Northern Ireland's focus on sectarian identities over other identities such as gender and race, combine to provide an ineffective and potentially harmful landscape to address the issue. It is clear that discussions on the intersection of race and gender in NI are in their infancy but the framing of these conversations around whiteness and its dominance in movements rather than only the inclusion of ethnic minority women is a positive step.

Considerations of intersectionality and race were also noted in thinking about models of good practice in gender equality. Northern Ireland has, by feminist activists and academics in the region, been highlighted for its negative record on both implementing policy on gender equality and achieving outcomes, when thinking about where NI could look to for inspiration in how to make better laws and policies, one participant observed:

When it comes to the places that are quite good for gender equality it's for white women ... like I mean even Sweden is moving to the right ... if you're a Black woman I don't think you're going to be saying it's great for gender equality.[12]

A commitment to intersectionality is part of a collective feminist identity in NI and this commitment goes beyond simply considering the inclusion of different groups of women into the feminist movement to recognise that power imbalances and open discussion of this power are part of the process of progressing inclusive feminist political spaces.

Networks and coalition building

The success of social movement building, and in achieving movement goals, can be found partially in the strength of networks within, and coalitions between, movements. Alliances within and among social movement groups are important to success and solidarity building across movements (Beamish and Luebbers, 2009). Networks can include the personal relationships which are built between activists within a movement to the relationships between movements built by actors who cross movements or those who consciously engage and build relationships with other groups. The strength of relationships within groups contributes to a strong collective identity and longer engagement while the relationships between groups can contribute to stronger social capital and more potential for influence and movement success (Tindall, 2023).

Coalition building occurs when distinct social movements agree to cooperate and work together towards a common goal whilst keeping a distinct identity (McCammon and Moon, 2014). Coalitions can be long or short term, potentially based around a particular event or reaction to threat, or enduring a more durable coalition which may result in an umbrella organisation forming with groups within it (Levi and Murphy, 2006). Some coalitions are seen to be more natural than others, for example, coalitions between the women's and LGBT+ movements are often predicated on shared ideologies and goals, along with bridges across movements with shared actors (Townsend-Bell, 2021). Previous research has found that when resources are high and a collective threat is imminent, movements are more likely to form coalitions and achieve success. This section considers how networks and coalitions have been built by the women's sector and feminist groups and the contribution towards movement building and identity.

Northern Ireland is a small place, both geographically and politically. Many participants mentioned that the size of Northern Ireland can often be a positive in terms of creating relationships and contacts with politicians and civil servants and that feminist actors can be trusted sources of information. This was noticed by the following participant in terms of groups who are anti-trans rights, in this instance referencing the UK group Sex Matters who advertised with billboards in advance of the 2022 elections 'Respect my sex if you want my X'.[13] Since Northern Ireland uses a proportional voting system (with votes ranked in numerical preference) the slogan makes less sense in this context. As this participant notes, groups were able to come together to let politicians know that this group was not supported by them and that the majority of its membership comes from outside Northern Ireland:

> We could see some of the anti-trans groups trying to get in here but because the politicians know a few of us, and know who we are, and we were able to come together and say, this is not a coming from us. Most of them are not based in Northern Ireland.[14]

This ability to mobilise quickly across groups is also reflected in the reaction to the 'Let Women Speak' demonstration in Belfast in April 2023. The group describes itself as pursuing women's sex-based rights and much of the group's actions appears to centre on the theme of same-sex spaces for women and to this end denying trans women access to these spaces.[15] In response to their event, LGBT+ groups, feminist groups, women's centres, trade unions and other community groups came together to organise a counter-demonstration in support of trans rights. The speed at which a broad range of groups could be brought together and the fact that the counter-demonstration was bigger than the demonstration indicates the ability to mobilise quickly in the face of threats and challenges to collective feminist identities.

The strength of the network of women's centres, organisations and feminist groups in NI has meant they are often invited to participate in policy-making spaces as experts (how this expertise is used and valued is discussed in the following chapter). This ability to be present in and influence policy-making spaces means that they are an important network for other groups to tap into. As one participant who works in the field of race and ethnic minority rights touched on:

> I think the fact that we now have so many connections in the women's sector has been hugely positive. The more connections we can make across sectors, groups working at the grassroots and advocating for people who are made vulnerable by intersecting structures, violent structures…like I said we've got into way more rooms than we would ever have been invited in before than ever before.[16]

In this way, the women's movement can act as a focal point or umbrella for other social movements as it already has the social capital to enter and influence formal political spaces. This is important, as formal politics in NI often operates on a zero-sum game approach, where rights given to one group must be taken away from another. Without a strong network and coalition building it is possible that rights can be weaponised, with promises of rights to one group at the expense of another. One participant explained that with some strong political opposition to abortion rights, a bargain was proposed in which same-sex marriage and an act governing the use of the Irish language in public office were to be offered at the expense of abortion rights:

> Whenever Stormont was scrambling to come back, there was rumours that they were going to allow, you know, equal marriage, and maybe Irish language at the expense of abortion. And so that joint statement came out from all three organisations, saying, our rights are to be played off against each other. So, even though those are all very different things, it was about overarching human rights.[17]

Solidarity between groups illustrates the indivisibility of rights and the ineffectiveness of attempts to play rights off one another. Solidarity and a collective feminist voice can also be shown across borders. Abortion rights in Northern Ireland and the Republic of Ireland changed dramatically almost in tandem. A successful referendum to repeal an amendment to the Irish Constitution banning abortion took place in May 2018 and the repeal of Sections 58–59 of the 1861 Offences Against the Person Act (OAPA) in Northern Ireland was voted in October 2019 in Westminster. In the run-up to the referendum activists from Northern Ireland organised and campaigned with their counterparts in the Republic of Ireland and the Alliance for Choice sits on the advisory board of the Irish Abortion Rights Campaign having a voice in larger discussions about strategies and approaches (Roberts, 2022). After changes in the Republic of Ireland, this solidarity was continued with support for the North, in particular the support of Irish diaspora groups such as the London-Irish Abortion Rights Campaign and their engagement with Stella Creasy, the Labour MP who brought forward the proposal to repeal the relevant sections of the OAPA (Sanquest, 2022).

Social media

Social media has been described as a defining feature of contemporary activism and of fourth wave feminism. The use of social media to communicate, organise and build movements and identities across larger geographical spaces is characterised by the speed of communication, the capacity to reach large numbers of people and the removal of the need for people to be in the same physical space (Caren et al., 2020). The use of social media to organise has been highlighted for its potential to flatten hierarchies in organising, allowing participation by broader groups of people and the emergence of new movements. However, it has also been critiqued for the shallowness of activism, the term 'clicktivism' or 'slacktivism' and that it may enable more surveillance of groups (Storer and Rodriguez, 2020). Online spaces, like any space, are gendered. For women, participating in online spaces, anonymity enables a high probability of threats of violence and abuse. However, the ability to use online spaces, which can be less intimidating than physical meetings, to find feminist groups and begin discovering a feminist identity is an important part of bringing people into movement building.

An example of the power of social media but also its complexities can be seen in the example of online activism on gender-based violence, in particular the example of #MeToo. The 'MeToo' hashtag became globally known in October 2017 after American actress Alyssa Milano used it. Within one month it had been used 1.7 million times across eighty-five countries to document experiences of sexual abuse and harassment. As such it can be described as one of the most publicised and global online movements of recent times. This connectivity and ability to share common experiences is incredibly important to engage public consciousness and build momentum around a movement but at the same time those involved in such activism report how labour-intensive and emotionally draining it is, the risks of encountering online abuse also become higher after telling one's story publicly. In terms of intersectionality in movement building, as highlighted earlier, online spaces, whilst enabling more accessibility, continue to elevate certain voices over others and could be described as reinforcing particular power relations. The point has been made frequently that the person who developed the term, African American activist Tarana Burke, has rarely been seen as the face of the movement and arguments have been made that there is racial bias in terms of how victims are perceived and how much attention is given to white women over Black women (Phipps, 2021).

Online feminist spaces can be important forums to share ideas, learn the vernacular of a movement and, of course, to share details of in-person meetings. In Northern Ireland, the Belfast Feminist Network group which started as a loose collective of feminists in 2010, started a Facebook page which to date has almost five thousand followers. This page is moderated by volunteers, all of whom do this in their spare time. As the group became more popular and more comments were being posted this created discussion and debate a lot of which had to be moderated for offensive or problematic content. Participants who had been involved in this work noted how labour-intensive it became:

But then people started saying things like, you know we reported this, and you haven't done anything, and it's been a day. And like this is nobody's job. People in the Facebook group started saying things like 'this isn't very professional', and I was thinking to myself, if you complain to a company, you would be getting a response like in ten working days, or whatever. But people were like sort of saying 'You're not responding fast enough' all that sort of thing. And then, when people were removed from the group, they would message and complain about being removed and we would tell them 'You were warned, and we have rules for a reason'. So yeah, it just became too much hassle, whereas at the start I think it was good, and but that's because it was a mixture of people, not that everybody came to meetings or came to events, but there was more, a bigger proportion of people who did. And then, as it grew and grew, it was people who didn't know each other, you know it was that sort of people didn't have a like a personal connection. So it's easier to be rude to someone. It's also easier to misconstrue what somebody's saying.[18]

The quote above highlights the problems with online spaces as they become more popular and increasing numbers join. Online space can give a distorted view of the actual participation in a movement, as participants noted whilst one to two hundred people can say they will attend an event, often this means around 10–20 per cent of this number will actually be there. When people do not have relationships in person, this also makes it easier to call out people rather than recognising that many people may be coming to feminism for the first time and learning new ways to think and speak about topics. Whilst moderators would delete and occasionally block those who did this, it is impossible to monitor a page constantly. In this way, online space can become alienating for some approaching feminism for the first time and may discourage participation in face-to-face events. Campbell and Roberts (2024) write about this labour with regard to social media and abortion activism in NI. The design of multiple social media accounts and the creation of content in the form of 'community education, stigma busting and lobbying' (Campbell and Roberts, 2024: 9) alongside monitoring and updating these accounts, amounts to a huge amount of invisible labour, mostly undertaken by volunteers. Trolling and online abuse are an additional layer to this labour and arise prominently in feminist and pro-choice online spaces.

Whilst the Belfast Feminist Network page has currently become more of a space to share information and news items, it was highlighted that when there are public instances of discrimination or harm it can become a forum to provide a cohesive response and united front. During the period of what is referred to as the Ulster rugby rape trial,[19] there was intense public and media interest and also upset and outrage from those who felt the coverage of the trial was misogynistic. At this time, it was viewed as important to have a feminist space where views could be shared and responses coordinated:

> We don't try and maintain it as a community anymore, because there are other communities in Belfast. Now what we have maintained, is a platform where we can say things that other organizations don't necessarily say...and that's worked really well in terms of the public discourse, and being a platform that you know we can take contentious things to the media. So, the last time for me, was around the Ulster Rugby trial where all the women's groups and organizations that were involved in that were getting a lot of backlash and a lot of media attention. So, under the banner BFN, I did all of the media for the protests around the court.[20]

Online space became particularly important for the ongoing work of movements during waves of the COVID-19 pandemic. When pandemic prevention policy meant that people were not allowed to meet in person, online space became integral to maintaining ongoing work and continuing movement building. Deiana et al. (2022), write that feminists in NI were particularly adept at responding to crisis, as this is a regular part of dysfunctional politics in NI. However, in the post-pandemic period, several participants highlighted that they worried that the shift to organising online had meant that some people struggled with coming back into face-to-face spaces and this could mean bringing new people into the feminist movement was more of a challenge:

> the other challenges for me, as I said, I think that it's always the same people who may be organising and perhaps this this may be one of the effects of the pandemic, I feel the fact that without meeting in person, I think it becomes more difficult to recruit, you know, to get more people on board.[21]

Online space may provide some of the interaction needed to create a collective feminist identity but if this is not translated into regular interaction in organising it will not contain the momentum to keep negotiating and renegotiating these collective identities through the involvement of wider groups of people.

Conclusions

The formation of a collective identity is a central aspect of creating a distinct political space and voice for the feminist movement. Examining Northern Ireland through the lens of contemporary features of feminist identity, the role of intersectionality, coalitions and networks and social media, helps to situate NI within global feminist movement building. Yet the role of context and the specific social, cultural and political background of NI remains important in distinguishing it from other feminist movements. Difference has always been part of feminist organising in NI, this has predominantly focused on the question of constitutional status and how it is to be negotiated within the movement. Historically, this has at times resulted in a neutral position or in the adoption of transversal strategies for dialogue and engagement. As conversations continue about the future of the island of Ireland, it is necessary for a diversity of feminist perspectives to enter this conversation.

The size of NI enables strong coalitions and networks to emerge, feminist groups and the women's sector are in a good position to lead and harness such networks due to their strong collective identity and recognition within wider political spaces. This ability to reach across differing social movements also enables a strong collective voice and identity on human rights and means that when rights claims may be used to try and divide movements, there is little chance of this strategy working.

Locating feminism in NI to the global feminist literature there is a strong commitment to intersectionality but, of course, realising this in practice is a constant process of negotiation and consideration of power relations. It is recognised that there is ongoing work needed on this front, but that this process needs to recognise power and privilege beyond inclusion. The role of social media in developing a collective identity also throws up problems of inclusion and how to ensure that whilst maintaining a safe space people are able to explore issues that they may be coming to for the first time. There is also the global issue of translating online engagement into face-to-face organising.

The strength of the feminist movement in NI and its development of a strong collective identity where activists commit to many of the core features of contemporary global feminist organising but considered within the framework of the background to NI and its continual negotiation of difference has a lot to tell feminist movements globally. Where legacies of conflict may have minimised or invisibilised these stories and movement building, they provide a strong narrative for the consideration of differences in feminist political spaces.

Notes

1 This refers to a trial in 2018 where Ulster Rugby players were accused of rape and found not guilty. The verdict was followed by protests in the North and

Republic of Ireland against the verdict. The trial was widely publicised, in particular many of the rape myths that were put forward by the defence barristers. An overview of the trial and public reaction can be found here: https://www.theguardian.com/news/2018/dec/04/rugby-rape-trial-ireland-belfast-case (last accessed 12/02/2025).
2 https://www.reclaimtheagenda.com/ (last accessed 12/02/2025).
3 The Easter Rising was a six-day armed insurrection in 1916 against British rule by Irish Republicans.
4 Interview 8, 2022.
5 Interview 7, 2022.
6 The Holy Cross dispute occurred in 2001 and 2002 in Ardoyne in north Belfast. Holy Cross Primary School, an all-girls Catholic school was located in a predominantly Protestant area. In 2001, Loyalists began picketing the school, claiming that Catholics were regularly attacking their homes and denying them access to facilities. They blocked the route to the school and the protests gained international media attention as some protestors threw bricks, stones and urine-filled balloons at the children and their parents.
7 In 2012, Belfast City Council voted to limit the days that the Union Flag flies from Belfast City Hall. The vote reduced the flying of the flag from every day to 18 days a year, the minimum requirement for UK government buildings. For months after, this resulted in protests by Unionists and Loyalists which have been ongoing since but have reduced in numbers and frequency.
8 https://herloyalvoice.com/ (last accessed 12/02/2025).
9 Interview 17, 2022.
10 Interview 13, 2022.
11 Interview 4, 2022.
12 Interview 14, 2022.
13 https://sex-matters.org/ (last accessed 12/02/2025).
14 Interview 8, 2022.
15 https://www.standingforwomen.com/events (last accessed 12/02/2025).
16 Interview 12, 2022.
17 Interview 7, 2022.
18 Interview 23, 2022.
19 See endnote 1.
20 Interview 9, 2022.
21 Interview 4, 2022.

3

Gender experts, participation and policy making

Feminist engagement in formal political processes in Northern Ireland has resulted in some moments of success, in particular the inclusion of women within negotiations to the Agreement. However, these moments of success are rare and the commitments made, for example the right to women's political participation or the inclusion of civil society in formal politics in the form of a Civic Forum, have not been fully realised. The male domination of institutions and the marginalisation of gender and feminist issues within political domains has bred frustration but not disengagement from these institutions and policy making processes. Feminist actors continue to build relationships, evidence, strategies and networks to engage with state processes and ensure that gender and feminist perspectives on issues are put forward in public debate and the political domain.

This chapter considers how gender and gender expertise operate in formal political and policy making spaces. In particular, the chapter interrogates how feminist actors can work to influence and shape these spaces and if it is possible to make tangible feminist change in male-dominated political spaces which give primacy to ethno-national identity. In this chapter, I am engaging with the work of feminist actors in consultative forums including, for example, the working group for the NI Gender Equality Strategy or the All-Party Group on Women, Peace and Security, political spaces where the women's sector and feminist actors are specifically consulted and invited to provide their expertise. In addition, I will consider the spaces where gender expertise is not considered relevant and therefore excluded.

It is apparent that outside of explicitly gendered political issues certain bodies, voices and experiences can be excluded from forums because gender is not considered integral to knowledge and policy making in these areas. Intersectionality, explored in the last chapter, is not often understood in formal politics. Feminist actors have fought to be included in policy making spaces, yet how their gender expertise is understood, utilised and acted on (or not) needs consideration in evaluating the outcomes of such engagements. The aim of this chapter is to interrogate the tensions and progressions that occur when those who have expert gender knowledge and feminist political goals are in political spaces to inform policy making and the tangible results of this inclusion (or exclusion).

The rise of gender experts and expertise has been explored globally with a vast literature that addresses what these actors do, the effects that they have and if gender expertise can be considered in tune with feminist values in terms of the type of change that happens and the professionalisation of knowledge. These ideas are woven into this chapter and contribute towards an understanding of the complexity of trying to translate feminist vernacular and understandings of gender inequality into local institutionalised contexts where understandings of gender and limited and narrow. Overall, the chapter concludes that whilst it is important to be invited and participate in these spaces, and that feminist actors have done immense work in contributing to these spaces, a frustration can emerge in translating ideas into action. Frustration results in a weariness and wariness expressed by gender experts that their work in policy-building can have any transformative effect.

Feminism, the state and gender experts

The relationship, or if there should be a relationship, between feminism and the state can most accurately be described as contested terrain. The state can be viewed as both a key site of the reproduction of gender inequality and injustice and also the site to contest and remove this inequality and injustice. Within feminist activism there is an argument that feminist work and transformative action can only be taken outside of formal institutions and structures, or that feminist actors can only remain critical when distanced from the state. The suspicion of the male-dominated patriarchal state and its potential co-option and dilution of feminism, has been discussed in more recent debates about abolitionist feminism, which rather than advocating for a distanced relationship with the state, proposes that the state and its institutions should be dismantled and replaced with community-based structures and organisation (see for example, Davis et al., 2022).

At the same time, feminist actors have worked within state structures providing advocacy, expertise and critical friendship. As Chappell (2000) has noted, movement away from a binary understanding of the state as either being inherently patriarchal or benign can be more productive and allow for consideration of the relationship between gender and the state, opportunities that arise, and how feminist actors shape this relationship in different times and places. Chappell highlights that considering both structures and agents can help us understand the relationship between feminism and the state or factors which will make this interaction successful. This chapter, rather than engaging in an ideological debate about whether feminist actors should engage with the state, will explore and analyse the relationship that women's movement actors have with the state and the ways in which this contributes to gendered policy making. As such the question is reframed as to the utility of engaging with state institutions and policy-making mechanisms.

State feminism is simply the advocacy of women's movement demands inside the state (Lovenduski, 2005: 4). Actions are often taken through women's policy machineries or institutional mechanisms for the advancement of women, set up to advance gender equality or gender mainstreaming in policy. Research documenting the success of women's movement actors in state institutions has been found to be a combination of a high level of institutionalisation of such groups coupled with more moderate levels of activism. In short, the more established a group is the more likely it is to be included in the policy arena (Sauer and Wöhl, 2011). However, the success of state feminism has been questioned by gender scholars, as Celis and Childs (2020) state:

> to conclude that contemporary electoral politics fails to address the representational needs of women should not invite serious scholarly criticism; it is empirically verifiable. To restate: women's issues are frequently far down the political agenda, and those that are included in party programs and do find themselves at the center of political debate do not necessarily reflect the priorities of women, more specifically, the women most affected by them ... similarly, the establishment of gender machinery and women's policy agencies is frequently constrained by their political contexts and again has found it hard to feminize the political agenda. (Celis and Childs, 2020: 158)

The representation of 'women's' or 'gender' interests can come from a wide range of actors and goes beyond elected representatives. This engages with ideas of collective identity building, with concerns being articulated through negotiation rather by a singular actor. This interaction will be more effective at allowing needs to be defined from evidence and from grassroots women's groups rather than being imposed from the top-down. The ability for feminist engagement in policy making to make tangible change has been questioned. Sara Ahmed's (2007) analysis arises from the perspective of contributing to racial equality and EDI policies in UK universities and focuses on the purpose of these documents and the role of academics as experts who contribute and sign off on them. Ahmed writes that these documents are seen to make claims about institutions, that they are diverse or anti-racist and point towards future action to enable these goals, but that in many cases 'doing the document' is where action ends, the document becomes an end in itself. In many ways those who are involved in providing experience and expertise in drafting these documents become compliant and complicit as they are seen to provide credibility for the document.

Chappell and MacKay (2021: 171) present a more hopeful approach to the research and analysis of institutions. They describe the approach of feminist actors as 'chipping away rather than sweeping away' with the sense that change happens incrementally but can add up to larger transformational shifts. They advocate for looking to the everyday interactions and tensions within institutions. Eschle and Maiguashca (2018) advise moving away from a binary understanding of bad and good feminists. They describe the 'bad girl' as those who are co-opted into working with neoliberal institutions being pitted against the 'good girl' i.e., those who resist the neoliberal co-option of feminism. They argue that narratives of co-option and resistance of feminism have become so binary that they lose nuance and that paying attention to the experiences of those feminists working in these spaces would be a more productive way of teasing out the specifics, tensions and paradoxes of doing such work.

A shift to insider politics by women's movement in Western democracies began in the 1980s (Sauer and Wöhl, 2011). This came in parallel with the women's movement moving from informal to more formal groups indicating institutionalisation of the movement. The rise of specialised knowledge about gender in policy making arose largely out of the centralising of gender mainstreaming in international development policy in the 1990s and subsequently through international policies such as the UN Women, Peace and Security agenda. The work of gender experts ranges from changing institutional and organisational practices, including gender considerations into various issue areas and policies through to training and project planning (Kunz and Prügl, 2019). Alongside the international sphere there has been a rise in gender expertise in national spheres, for example, in Australia the term 'femocrat' was coined in the 1990s to describe this phenomenon (Eisenstein, 1996) whilst in the UK it has been described as 'professional feminist' (Ross, 2019). Ross's work on local governance in the 1980s and the work of the Women's Liberation Movement within this describes a professional feminist as someone with 'feminist knowledge of gender inequality; their paid "challenge position" in relation to the ideas and organising of their institutional location; and their motivation to bring practical change to people's lives' (527). She indicates that this role blurs the line between a social movement and the state.

There are a broad range of actors considered gender experts. Hoard (2015: 12) provides a comprehensive definition of a gender expert as '(1) an individual with feminist knowledge regarding the cause-and-effect relationship between policies, actions, and/or activities and gender inequalities, and who (2) is formally requested to provide her knowledge and services'. Lovenduski (2007) uses the helpful term 'feminist policy network' to encompass politicians, women's movement actors and policy agencies. These definitions move away from the paid nature of the work and a need to be explicitly working 'for' the state rather than 'with' it on a consultancy basis. The insider/outsider status is relevant to Northern Ireland, as there is no formal women's equality machinery within the state with the Equality Commission acting for all strands of equality duties (with sectarianism taking precedence), and as noted earlier the Civic Forum, developed through the Agreement, has rarely been active.

Feminists working with the state have to engage with differing understandings and interpretations of gender equality and tensions arise in how feminists can translate their understandings into government policy. Critiques of state feminism have indicated that it can result in ideas being diluted or turned into tick box exercises which give a sense of progress whilst depoliticising feminist ideas. Nancy Fraser has described this co-option and depoliticization of feminist ideas as feminism entering a dangerous liaison with neo-liberalism unwittingly making feminism capitalisms handmaiden. This process has meant the feminist politics of redistribution being overshadowed by the politics of recognition, which she views to have elevated cultural concerns over those of socio-economic redistribution (Fraser, 2013). Rottenberg (2014) argues that this intertwining of feminism and neo-liberalism works to individualise women and focus on their ability to take part in the workforce rather than promote collective action and solidarity. In these visions of feminist engagement with the state, policy actions become about benefitting a small cohort of women as individuals rather than as a collective group.

How gender equality is interpreted in policy making can be viewed through the lens of 'stretching' and 'shrinking' (Lombardo, Meier and Verloo, 2009). Shrinking of gender equality narrows the meaning to focus on a formal definition of equality or simply non-discrimination whereas stretching expands the definition to substantive equality or to see links with other identity factors. How these are interpreted into policy can be described as processes which involve 'tinkering' with policy to achieve equal treatment, 'tailoring' situations to the needs of women or 'transformative' policies in which new standards for everyone can transform the gendered nature of institutions (Benschop and Verloo, 2006). Benschop and Verloos analysis in the context of a Belgian Ministry illustrates how attempts to integrate gender equality whilst resulting in some successful actions and a greater legitimacy to gender equality work can be hindered by attempts to water down or neutralise feminist ideas making it difficult to reach transformative potential.

Currently, there has been a move by states to go further than labelling policy gender-sensitive to explicitly labelling it as feminist. This has most commonly been seen with feminist foreign policy, states such as Sweden, Canada, France and Mexico have labelled their foreign policy feminist since 2015. Academics researching this development have asked the question if labelling policy making feminist goes beyond depoliticised ideas of gender equality and moves towards a more radical understanding (Aggestam et al., 2019). Analysis of these documents has illustrated an 'empowerment as efficiency' and 'empowered women as leaders' approach, the documents also function as a way for states to promote a form of feminist nationalism whereby they signal themselves to be part of a liberal international order and furthers these states position on the global stage (Thomson, 2020). Importantly, when we talk about including feminism in policy making, it must be kept in mind that there are multiple forms of feminism. Understandings of gender equality can often revolve around homogenous understandings of women and their interests and an approach which favours liberal feminist norms such as inclusion of women rather than transformation of institutions.

Of course, the relationship between the state and feminism must begin by feminists being invited into the room. Nirwal Puwar (2004) uses the term 'space invaders' to describe the people who aren't seen to be the norm within positions of leadership and therefore are not viewed to have authority, expertise or legitimacy in these spaces. Whilst theoretically, everyone has the right to enter political space, some bodies are marked as not fitting. However, this position does not foreclose the potential for change, spaces are dynamic, open to possibilities and shifts, and as their occupants change there is potential for contestation and transformation. When women enter formal political spaces, whether as elected representatives or to provide their expertise, they are entering as gendered subjects. Historical and contemporary gendered power relations must be considered in how they negotiate these spaces and the influence they can have. Considering participation and potential for change, Iris Marion Young (2000) refers to external and internal inclusion. External inclusion is the ability to join the decision-making forum whilst internal inclusion indicates a tangible opportunity to influence others and, consequently, to influence the result. This may also be described as equality of presence and equality of voice (Smith, 2009; Wojciechowska, 2022).

One of the barriers to both forms of inclusion is that those entering spaces have to be identified as having relevance in the space. Whilst some issues will be labelled as explicitly gendered, others may not be and so 'proving' relevance to be both present and heard will add extra layers of complexity to the process. In the Northern Ireland example, this has been highlighted consistently with regard to issues of peacebuilding, memory, security and policing. These issues are perceived to affect communities primarily on the axis of ethno-national identity, with gendered experience being understood as either secondary or possibly dangerous as it may disrupt hegemonic narratives and enable commonalities to be recognised between these communities (Pierson, 2017, 2018b). More recently, on the issue of the future constitutional status of Northern Ireland, Fidelma Ashe (2024) has written of how whilst women may be invited to contribute to these discussions there may be little consideration of gender issues unless they are explicitly written into the design of discussions. Women will also have to negotiate intersecting identity markers, such as class, in having their claims heard.

A zero-sum game, or ideologically pure, approach to feminist action is unhelpful in a political climate characterised by continual crisis. Links between the state and feminism are currently under attack. Globally, there is a backlash against women's rights under the guise of combatting 'gender ideology', states such as the United States, Brazil and Poland have utilised this framing to stand against norms of gender equality both in local and global forums. In the UK context, research has pointed towards a link between men perceiving themselves to be discriminated against and votes for Brexit (Green and Shorrocks, 2023). The concerted campaign against trans and non-binary people's rights in the UK also points towards an increasing slide to far right politics and the co-option of feminist ideas such as the protection of women for anti-feminist ends (Phipps, 2021). In this climate, understanding how feminists interact with the state, how understandings of gender equality are negotiated in these forums and how progress is made, is vitally important with the very real potential for backsliding of gains already made.

Gender, policy making and substantive representation in NI

Within literature on consociational power-sharing there has been feminist consideration of the exclusion of women and the privileging of ethno-national identity over other identity cleavages (Kennedy et al., 2016). This literature addresses how the privileging of ethno-nationalism can prioritise a particularly conservative gender order for women and deprioritise gender concerns within post-conflict environments. As described in Chapter 1, whilst descriptive representation of women has risen in the NI Assembly it continues to be a heavily masculinised space with conservative and traditional views and attitudes towards women's roles in society, to the conduct of politics and towards women within politics. Whilst the numbers of women may rise in a particular institution, the gendered institutional dynamics of the institution may take longer to shift and change (MacKay and Murtagh, 2019; Ní Aoláin, 2018).

It is argued that within consociationalism further consideration needs to happen on where, why and how the substantive representation of women occurs (Gavrić, 2024). Definitions of substantive representation begin with Hannah Pitkin's understanding of acting in the interest of the represented, in a manner responsive to them (Pitkin, 1967). Within women's substantive representation, women's interests can be defined in a narrow, prescriptive way or can be viewed to be contextually located and dependent on social, political and temporal factors. Whether increased descriptive representation of women leads to better substantive representation is questionable, female politicians may not always act in the interests of women or wish to. This can be more overt in power-sharing regimes where ethno-national identity has primacy. This chapter takes a broader view of representation arguing that is not only elected representatives who can act for women but that the articulation of women's interests by feminist actors and women's groups who work as gender experts within policy making may better represent women's interests and help to effect more substantive change for women.

How gender equality is considered within law and policy making is dependent on the structures which govern equality. The Agreement provided several in-roads to advance gender equality in law and policy making. Part of these were contained within the Northern Ireland Act (NIA) 1998 (British legislation designed to give effect to the Agreement). Part VII was titled Human Rights and Equal Opportunities and Section 75 establishes the grounds on which public authorities have a statutory duty of due regard to promote equality of opportunity. The categories included in this duty are between persons of different religious beliefs, political opinion, racial group, age, marital status or sexual orientation; between men and women generally; between persons with a disability and persons without; and between persons with caring responsibility for dependents and persons without. As such, the potential of this legislation laid the grounds for state transformation of gender relations. However, this commitment has not played out in practice, in part due to misinterpretations of equality as formal equality of opportunity rather than equality of outcome and a form of 'punitive equality' (Roulston quoted in Cockburn, 2013) where positive discrimination towards women has been challenged.

Equality has also been relegated in a hierarchy with community relations. Section 76 of the NIA, which deals with religious equality between Catholic and Protestant communities, is legally enforceable whereas the legal enforceability of Section 75, dealing with other equalities, depends on the specific circumstances of the case.[1] This hierarchy between equality duties has been seen in subsequent agreements and community relations policy where women have been almost erased from texts. Analysis of the effects of Section 75 have found it to be reduced in many circumstances to a 'tick-box' exercise with procedural duties overriding commitment to effectiveness in practice (ECNI, 2003). The Agreement also set the conditions for the creation of the Northern Ireland Human Rights Commission and the creation of a Bill of Rights for Northern Ireland. This process is still ongoing with drafts presented but not accepted, and to date NI does not have a Bill of Rights. Draft Bills of Rights have included provisions on gender-based violence but no provisions on abortion or same sex marriage.

More recent accounts of gender policy making have pointed towards an ambivalent approach to gender and feminist issues within the Northern Ireland Assembly. Thomson (2017) writes that whilst there appears to be no opposition to liberal feminist norms such as women's participation these are not acted on in concrete ways to create gender friendly policies. Research on gender policy illustrates a gender neutral or blind approach to policy making and proofing. It appears that policy is proofed via a formal approach to treating men and women the same which does not result in equal outcomes, or substantive equality for women (Gray et al., 2020). Formal understandings of equality divorce gender from its historical and contemporary context and ignore the material inequality for women in society. There is also a further lack of identifying gender concerns in policy, for example, the current Draft Programme for Government does not reference gender equality and there is a lack of data on gender inequalities and outcomes (Gray et al., 2020). Whilst the Executive Office collected and published data on gender inequality between 2008 and 2015 this data stopped being collected in 2015 when responsibility for gender equality moved to the Department for Communities (Rouse et al., 2023). Rouse (2016) argues that the lack of delivery on gender equality can be attributed to benign institutional resistance from conservative civil servants or a more malign resistance to implementation at the top. It is clear, however, that there is a lack of budgeting to ensure gender equality is reached.

Beyond formal approaches to gender equality and a lack of data at the institutional level there continues to be a lack of progress on development of policies which would tangibly effect women and progress action on gender equality. NI's Gender Equality Strategy expired in 2016 and whilst there has been consultation with an expert panel and a co-design group with recommendations produced in 2020 (Gray et al., 2020) there continues to be no current Gender Equality Strategy. Northern Ireland is the only region of the UK without a childcare strategy (see Conclusion for further consideration of care policy) and also the only region without a specific women's health strategy. Whilst in 2021 the Executive Office began the process of drafting a Strategic Framework to End Violence Against Women and Girls the consultation period on this document only ended in October 2023 and a policy is not currently in place. Women's Aid, a lead agency on domestic abuse had their core funding cut by the NI Department of Health in September 2023, threatening the future of service provision.[2] Whilst abortion was decriminalised by Westminster in October 2019, the Department of Health refused to commission services resulting in the Secretary of State having to step in to ensure the provision of services (Pierson, 2022).

McLaughlin (2005) warned of the particular difficulties of law and policy making under the devolved Stormont regime, naming it a 'lowest common denominator' approach which would result in stagnancy and socially conservative policies. This was reinforced by Gray and Birrell (2012) who found evidence of difficulty agreeing in some instances even on a lowest common denominator leading to a failure in policy development and falling behind standards in the rest of the UK. This lack of agreement can also be explained through the 'zero sum game' approach which typifies the majority of ethno-national politics in the region, where each gain is seen as a loss for the 'other side', leading to a lack of consensus or progressive policy creation. Under this regime, changing law and policy on even uncontested issues can be difficult. Hagen et al. (2022) also points to the difficulty of gender neutrality in recognising trans identities suggesting to policy makers that framing policies in the language of 'women and gender-minorities' can help to be inclusive whilst recognising the need to challenge barriers that gender can enforce in law.

Gender expertise and the women's sector in NI

The breadth of gender expertise in NI can be viewed through the lens of the particularly strong community sector in the region. The community and voluntary sector in Northern Ireland became prominent during the political vacuum of conflict and the history of women's community organising can be traced back to a failure to act on socio-economic inequality and service provision during the Troubles (Deiana, 2013). This is in line with many other conflicted societies where women are often pushed out of formal politics in conflict/post-conflict settings with their work taking place within civil society and in largely grassroots organisations (Pierson and Thomson, 2018). Women's groups can use their expertise to influence formal political processes and to ensure that gendered perspectives are included within political talks and peace agreements. Many members of the Northern Ireland Women's Coalition came from the community and voluntary sector (Fearon, 1999), in the early 1990s, in what would later become Bosnia-Herzegovina, a Women's Lobby was formed to encourage political parties to address women's needs in areas such as employment and healthcare (Cockburn, 1998) and in Burundi women's consistent efforts (despite great resistance) ensured an all-women's negotiation session, which was able to 'engender' the peace agreement (Anderson, 2016).

In 1992, the Opsahl Commission was commissioned to undertake a thirteen-month review to understand the experiences of, and possible solutions to, conflict through the voices of the Northern Irish people. Women who participated highlighted the role of women as agents of positive change through their work in the voluntary and community sector, in fact this was noted by the Commission to be one of the most positive areas of growth within the wider political arena (Opsahl Commission, 1993). Due to the very real structural and cultural constraints within formal politics, many women have attempted to claim political space within areas of informal politics in the form of grassroots, voluntary and community organisations. Whilst the women's sector is well organised and highly active, there has been a continued struggle to gain traction in the formal political sphere (Thomson, 2017). In 2014, 75 per cent of paid positions in the community and voluntary sector were held by women.[3] The history of organising in Northern Ireland, has created strong networks and innovative strategies as noted by Deiana et al. (2022: 2) with regard to the response to COVID-19, 'precisely because of a longstanding history of feminist organizing in a complex political and economic terrain, grassroots organizations have developed important strategies and situated knowledge to navigate this moment'.

The deficiencies of service provision led to a growth of networks and community-based groups which provided an alternative political space for women outside of formal politics. These networks rather than a formalised women's movement were less ideologically motivated and more of a response to material needs of communities, working on issues such as poverty, housing, employment and education. Whilst this work is obviously political work, the women's sector has been considered less as political actors but as service providers. Many of these groups may also not explicitly identify themselves as feminist whilst doing feminist work and have overtly avoided calling their work political, the aversion to naming the work of the women's sector as political can be traced back to strategies of transversal dialogue identified by Cockburn in the 1990s (Cockburn, 1998). Here, politics is directly connected to constitutional questions which groups may want to avoid, in part to ensure the continuance of funding and also to ensure the continuance of work across communities.

Part of this community is a strong network of women's centres with training, education and childcare facilities, largely located in communities most acutely affected by poverty and the legacy of the Troubles. Operating throughout Northern Ireland many were set up in the 1980s, often separated physically by community boundaries but linked together by broader base networks such as the Women's Resource and Development Agency,

Women's Support Network, Northern Ireland Rural Women's Network, Northern Ireland Women's Platform (previously the Northern Ireland Women's European Platform) and the Training for Women Network. Women's centres have often supported each other across traditional divides, the often-cited example is when the Falls Women's Centre (in a predominantly Nationalist community) was threatened with a withdrawal of funding from the Unionist dominated Belfast City Council their counterparts in the neighbouring Shankill Women's Centre (in a predominantly Unionist community) stood together with them to challenge the decision. This brought into being the Women's Support Network, an umbrella organisation of support networks for co-ordinators of women's centres and the Women's Education Project, now the Women's Resource and Development Agency. As Kellie Turtle (2013: 83) notes:

> the networks formed in the 1980s by way of mobilising women to engage in collective goals, have become key agencies in what is now a professional women's sector, campaigning for resources for the groups they represent and providing expert knowledge to policy makers required to address gender as part of their equality agenda.

The women's sector has been particularly effective in engaging with policy making processes both in terms of collecting evidence to inform policy-making and in gaining legitimacy within formal politics through extensive lobbying work. Within formal politics, there can be spaces that may prove more amenable to feminist interventions, within the Northern Ireland context in the post-Agreement era this was envisioned primarily to be through a venue such as the Civic Forum, which has had little opportunity for development. The Civic Forum was one of the propositions of the NIWC within the GFA. It was envisioned as a place where civil society could bridge the gap between communities and politicians and could provide recognition for the integral role that community-based organisations played in Northern Ireland for many years during the conflict. This space represents a participative mechanism allowing the co-operation of differing groups and especially those who may feel excluded from formal politics. In Northern Ireland, this would allow the vibrant civil society to share their knowledge and experience in the political sphere and in policy development. The Forum would ensure a more considered and deliberative approach to issues of policy and governance. It may facilitate those who are most marginalised from politics to have their voices heard through community representatives, women from the most socially and economically deprived areas, young women and women from ethnic minority backgrounds. Unfortunately, a lack of political will has meant that the Forum has not met since the suspension of the

Assembly in 2002. In April 2013, the Assembly voted to recall the Forum yet this decision is still to be enacted. The recent Fresh Start Agreement makes provision for a 'compact civic panel' of six members. Appointed directly by the First and Deputy First Ministers, they will be tasked 'to consider specific issues relevant to the Programme for Government'.

The failure of the Civic Forum illustrates the difficulty of enacting cross-community politics in which ethno-national identity is not embedded within the structure (Pierson and Thomson, 2018). The Civic Forum did not operate along the same logic of ethno-national primacy that the formal political structures had. As such, it was difficult for this very different understanding of politics and identity to link up with that understood by the Assembly. In addition, by its very existence, the Civic Forum required the formal political structures to cede part of their authority by acknowledging the Forum as a legitimate basis for politics and policy making. However, the Civic Forum provides an innovative blueprint for how civil society might be more effectively linked within formal consociational structures. Writing the existence of a Civic Forum more firmly into future peace agreements (for example, requiring it to have a formalised role in policy making) would help to more clearly entrench it within consociational structures, and force the formal political institutions to address it with greater seriousness.

The women's sector has also put immense effort into conducting research and collecting experiences from women all over Northern Ireland to contribute to collecting an evidence base for centring gender within wider policy discussions. With the outbreak of the COVID-19 pandemic in 2020 and the recognition that gender would be invisible in terms of who would be included within leadership committees (see below), the Women's Policy Group (a collection of those from the women's and human rights sector and feminist groups) came together to produce a comprehensive document, inspired by the Hawaiian Feminist COVID Recovery Plan,[4] that details how the post-pandemic recovery can be achieved through a gendered lens (Deiana et al., 2022). Similarly, the Women's Regional Consortium has recently produced a research report on how austerity measures have had a disproportionate impact on women. This report details both women's experiences of poverty and the gendered impact of austerity. Formed in 2013, after government departments identified a need for greater support for women in disadvantaged and rural areas, the Women's Regional Consortium is made up of representatives from the women's sector. These are just two recent examples of initiatives to collect evidence for change and are indicative of the fact that whilst the government is not collecting data on gender inequality there is a wealth of evidence which exists within the community sector to inform change.

Inclusion in political spaces

Before discussing the ways in which feminist actors work with and negotiate state institutions and policy making it is important to note that it is not in all cases that those actors are invited to the table to input their expertise. Whilst in policy making spaces where the subjects being discussed are explicitly gendered, expertise from the women's sector is sought, in other policy forums it is sometimes the case that minimal, or no women are in the room. Referring back to Young (2000) concept of internal (ability to influence policy) and external (the ability to join forums) inclusion, external inclusion remains a problem in Northern Ireland. Whilst there will be a strong consideration of parity in terms of ethno-national identity in the make-up of consultative forums, this often does not extend to other identity cleavages and indicates that legal enforceability may need to be extended to wider identity groups.

An example of this exclusion can be seen during the COVID-19 pandemic response. The pandemic brought into stark relief the gendered division of labour and the devaluation and invisibility of care labour with lockdowns and school and childcare closures and the intense pressure of the impossible balance of work and family life (Andrew et al., 2022). At this point, leaders and experts were convened by the Northern Ireland Executive to develop policies and a recovery plan, as many activists remarked there was an emergency leaders group set up for COVID-19 and there was no women's sector representative on it.[5]

The initial COVID-19 recovery plan developed by the Northern Ireland Executive had no women on its advisory panel and had very little mention of gender or care in its plan. Those in the women's sector had to lobby to be included in the leader's group and by this stage had taken inspiration from the Hawaiian approach and developed their own feminist COVID-19 recovery plan, as noted above. The exclusion of women in leadership and decision-making forums has been consistently noted in issues relating to peace, security and cultural legacies of conflict (Pierson, 2019). For example, a Commission on 'Flags, Identity, Culture and Tradition' appointed by the Office of the First Minister and Deputy First Minister in 2016 includes fourteen men and just one woman with no one on the panel having specific expertise in gender inequality. Whilst the final recommendations of the Commission refer to women, this is largely relating to Section 75 equality duties.[6] The lack of visibility of women in these deliberations ensure that women can see their experiences and opinions lack validity or relevance as 'experts' in the resolution of conflict in Northern Ireland.

Exclusion within formal and informal political spheres has a direct relationship. The exclusion of women as experts in some policy making forums extends to the wider political space of the community and voluntary sector, most notably the peacebuilding sector. As a participant in a previous project on gender security in Northern Ireland reported, with regard to those who are seen to be leaders in communities and who act as gatekeepers to the community:

> Oh yeah ... the gatekeepers ... they're always men ... I've never heard of a gatekeeper who's a woman. I mean there's still some very strong women out there who work with the strong personalities ... the men in the areas and they usually get on ok ... I can think of a couple of women's centres who have been able to work round situations but it's always men who are the gatekeepers or who are the group leaders who are saying you have to do this and there aren't any women who do that.[7]

The gatekeeping of women's community spaces has also extended, in some circumstances, to preventing women's groups from forming in certain communities (Pierson, 2015). The gatekeeping of women's groups and lack of visibility of women as community leaders means that when experts and leaders are being convened in policy making forums women end up being excluded from these spaces as they are not seen as legitimate voices and bodies. External and internal inclusion become intertwined as if women are not visible in these spaces at a community level (this does not mean they are not there, simply that they might not be the most visible) even if they do get a seat at the table, they may be less likely to be able to influence political and policy outcomes.

When feminist actors do get into formal political spaces to influence the creation of policy, they may need to change how they act or speak to fit themselves into these spaces. Puwar's (2004) concept of space invaders, where particular bodies are not seen to fit in political spaces, may see those traditionally excluded change their behaviour in order to fit the institutional context. For feminist actors engaging in policy making spheres, this was described as not being as forthright and using less radical language and tempering feminist ideas or framings:

> The overall goal is basically the same. But the methods you use might be different. When you're doing activist stuff you address issues in a more direct way, whereas with women's sector work you can get into spaces you couldn't otherwise get into, so you moderate your language a little bit, you moderate your tone.[8]

In this way as well as being a gendered body in a political space there is the added layer of being a feminist body. To gain legitimacy and some internal inclusion (the ability to influence outcomes) it may be necessary to act in a way that fits the institution, whilst this may allow for the use of language surrounding gender equality it may not go as far as accepting feminism or feminist framings of issues (this is discussed further in the following section).

The women's sector has also played a role in encouraging women's participation in electoral politics. Those who have worked in training women for elected roles emphasise that they focus on representation across the political spectrum. The participation of women in all political parties is based on arguments around ensuring representative democracy and draws on arguments including that made by Anne Phillips (1995) that whilst descriptive representation does not guarantee substantive representation it increases the possibilities of it. Organisations such as Women into Politics, DemocraShe and more recently 50:50 NI have worked with women across party lines (and with women who may not be aligned to a party yet) to provide training on the functioning of the electoral system in NI, media and public speaking training. Women who have taken this training are now elected representatives in a number of parties. Importantly, a pipeline issue has been identified between local government and the Assembly, as one participant explained:

> part of why male politicians were getting to level they were at, was because at local government level, you see it as part of a stepping stone to getting into the Assembly or getting into Westminster. But there are no resources for councils ... So at local government you work with council officers. So if all of the officers are male and most of the politicians are male, it kind of replicates itself.[9]

Local councils have also been encouraged through these training networks to adopt gender action plans and parties are encouraged to adopt a gender champion for local government. In this way, women's organisations encourage women's routes into formal politics and can also work through training to increase the potential for these representatives to consider issues of gender equality in law and policy making and also continue links between formal and informal politics through these relationships.

Talking different languages

Feminists engaging with the state often have differing interpretations and visions of gender equality than those they are working with. As described above this can involve narrow or formal interpretations of gender equality and these differing interpretations of what equality means will of course result in different solutions being offered. There is a need for feminists to engage in processes of translation and vernacularisation of their ideas into language that will be understood and appeal in differing policy spaces. Vernacularisation refers to processes whereby ideas are translated into a common language of understanding, with feminism and gender equality there is a need to find a common meaning with policy-makers so that proposed solutions work within this framework of understanding. This is a complex process as there is more than one form and understanding of feminism and results in tensions with meaning and communicating this meaning. As one participant identified:

> Policy people don't understand what gender equality means, do you know what I mean? Like they can have a very superficial understanding but they don't actually understand the norms and mechanisms where gender inequality is reproduced. So we need to explain what the problem actually is, why its happening before we offer them solutions.[10]

One of the key approaches to translating and adopting rights norms is 'framing', which is the interpretive package surrounding an idea. A theory of social movements, it analyses ways of packaging and presenting ideas which creates shared beliefs and motivates collective action. Butler's (2009) exploration of framing presents it as a means of controlling or defining the surrounding discourse, and consequently establishing the constraints of reality. The greater the resonance framing has with cultural traditions and narratives the more appealing it is said to be. However, Ferree (2003) reasons that often for activist groups, non-resonant discourses can be more politically radical, and accordingly have more potential for long-term social change, whereas resonant frames, although more successful in the short-term, may be required to sacrifice ideals and excludes certain groups and demands. In this way, framings that sit closer to policy-makers' understanding of gender equality may be more successful to deploy than more radical framings.

Within societies where a conservative gender order is prevalent, outside of feminist political spaces, understandings of women's agency and identity often revolve around particular tropes. One of the core features of women's identity in NI is that of motherhood. Framing issues of gender inequality through the lens of 'women and children' positions all women as mothers and protectors of children and appeals to a particular understanding of women in Northern Ireland. As the participant below states when speaking to politicians and policy-makers:

> So what we've done without really knowing we've done it is to say this is an operational issue. So you always have to pull back and reframe your argument I suppose, and that's how you win. But you're always doing that. With women it only works as even if it's clearly about women you then have to say

it's about children, it's not about women and you're always going to the next bit because they don't care about women. But I don't care, as it's the end that matters not the means, but you always have to go.[11]

Gender identities are reflective of power relations within society, in addition, political engagement and political agency also emanate from specific networks of power. Appealing to conservative narratives of female identity to make gains for women can be viewed as a challenge to sources of power by women, the ability to use conservative gender stereotypes for the benefit of women. However, this must be contrasted with its effect, which can be to re-establish and reinforce normative notions of femininity within the political sphere. In the longer term, this may help women become established in the political world but only within a very specific notion of agency revolving around traditional female traits and positions. As such, women who act outside these normative feminine frameworks may find themselves further marginalised. These framings aren't always translatable, for example, the mother/child argument is difficult to mobilise when advocating for abortion rights. However, conservative gender stereotypes can be strategically used to make gains for women. Traditional conservative gender narratives are understood and believed to be important by those in the largely male-led government and as such are a useful lobbying tool. Although this strategic use of identity is useful in the short-term for making political gains it may be problematic in the long-term by locating women's relationship with the state within conservative and narrow gender stereotypes.

Outside of feminist spaces, understandings of what feminism is or wants to achieve can be limited. Within policy making spheres there may be an assumption that women should advocate for a liberal 'lean-in' type of feminism, a policy which aims for women to break glass ceilings, achieving higher positions and increased income. From a feminist perspective, such a framing clearly puts value on certain types of work over others. Whilst for feminist actors, valuing care work both in and outside the home equally to other professions is an obvious framing and one where gender and class can be seen to intersect clearly, this framing may not be clear or resonant to a civil servant and, of course, involves a more complex solution than for example encouraging women into different professions. As one participant explained with regard to policy making on gender and workplace equality:

> So I was trying to explain – do you want a world where every woman is a scientist? Because if you want someone to mind your children while you're in the civil service working, pay those people because that's valuable work too. I was saying it at one point in frustration with tears in my eyes because it was the fifth time I'd explained it, gender inequality is rooted in valuing all

jobs equally because when we're talking about apprenticeships for women in STEM that's only one type of work and its paid well but other women are expected to do care work for free – why is that not valued?[12]

In the scenario above, the participant had attempted to explain multiple times that encouraging women into STEM[13] subjects will only benefit some women whilst valuing gendered jobs such as caring roles will benefit many more, if not all, women. However, valuing care work is a more complex process than for example creating gender apprenticeships or targets in STEM subjects, as such care is likely to be a less resonant frame within policy making. Valuing different forms of labour also requires an intersectional approach, what professions are considered skilled and subsequently well-paid is a question of both gender and class.

Understandings of gender equality lead us back to the first quote in this section, before presenting evidence and solutions, there is a role in talking through the roots of gender oppression and inequality and the ways in which this manifests and reproduces. Discussion of where gender inequality stems from is complex and has a variety of interpretations in feminism yet it is integral as a means to challenge dominant framings of gender equality and work towards solutions which stretch and transform policy rather than shrinking meanings or simply tinkering around the edges of inequality.

Compliance and slow progress

Public consultation on policy making has become an important tool in encouraging more horizontal forms of governance. For governments it is viewed as a useful tool for gathering views and targeting policies and for citizens it may be an important means to participate in decision-making. Consultation may also be a means to challenge or prevent democratic deficits, where the legitimacy of representative structures and processes are being called into question. There is increasing evidence that citizens want more transparent and participatory policy processes (Bishop and Davis, 2002). However, whether processes of consultation result in consumerist or empowered approaches to citizenship is contested (Cook, 2002). A consumerist approach is equated with the perception of involvement whilst decision makers retain power for themselves or legitimise controversial decisions through the lens of participation, whereas an empowered approach enables wider and deeper citizen involvement in decision-making.

Northern Ireland has been presented as 'unusually participatory by international standards' after the Agreement and as a result of it (Dubnick and Meehan, 2004: 7). Prior to this, under Direct Rule, governance fell to the Northern Ireland Office headed by the Secretary of State for Northern Ireland. Under this arrangement, governance was often undertaken by unelected bodies with limited local democracy or public accountability (Knox, 1998). Mechanisms included within the Agreement such as the Civic Forum or equality duties for public bodies such as Section 75 of the NIA, whilst designed to include greater means of participation have not necessarily reflected this goal in practice. Research conducted on consultation processes in NI has shown that policy-makers see public consultation as firstly a means of complying with statutory duties and, second to this, as a means to improve service delivery and best practice (Murray et al., 2009). Government officials involved in this research, whilst keen to collect a range of views, acknowledged that this may create 'unrealistic expectations' on how much participation could influence outcomes. Community groups' responses were similar, in that they often felt that consultation was a tick-box exercise and that decisions had been made in advance (Murray et al., 2009).

The suspicion highlighted in the previous paragraph, that consultation may be an exercise in statutory duty rather than a means to diversify policy processes and make them truly participatory was reiterated by participants in this research. One of the reasons that feminists may hesitate to engage with the state is that there is a perception that their ideas will be diluted or co-opted in formal policy documents and strategies. As described earlier, Ahmed (2007) reflects that critical actors can be used to legitimise a particular policy or position when that may not necessarily reflect their position or be brought into reality, she calls this 'doing the document'. In this sense, policy making becomes a performative process and consultation a legitimatising process. There was a sense of this from participants to the research, that at times the remit of policy had been decided in advance and there was a distinct limit to what ideas could be included or advanced. Subsequently, the expertise of the women's sector is recognised when it comes to gender equality issues but this participation may not make best use of the expertise given simply lending legitimacy to government policy:

> They're chipping away at the very point of what gender equality is, and sometimes they're only talking to you so they can get you rubber stamp something they've already decided to do in at least half the cases. Yeah, it's a real devaluation of expertise. And then who we count as experts is so narrow. Yeah, because you get invited to the space. So you must be considered an expert. But then to have that expertise just sort of thrown back in your face.[14]

In addition to a sense of devaluation of expertise as expressed by the participant above, there is a sense of consultation fatigue among feminist actors in NI. Consultation fatigue can come from the volume of consultations, the amount of documentation and the time-consuming nature of responding. The women's sector has collected a wealth of evidence from different pieces of research and consultation processes yet each new potential policy asks for more collection of evidence and specific responses. Many expressed a weariness with the constant need to respond or collect new evidence when it already existed and that policy didn't seem to move forward:

> That's the frustration for a lot of us in the sector, because change is so slow, and we feel like we've been saying the same things consultation after consultation, I've been saying the same things for decades and its like banging your head against a brick wall.[15]

> I think it (policy consultations) might be used as a mechanism to not do things, because all the evidence already exists. I'm not sure why we need to keep collecting more evidence.[16]

As detailed above whilst consultation exercises and recommendations have been made on policies, such as the Gender Equality Strategy and on a Strategic Framework to End Violence Against Women and Girls, these policies have not come to fruition contributing to a sense of frustration with the policy-making process. Without progress or a feedback loop on policy progression, trust is eroded in the policy making process. Lack of action on consultation processes and 'consultation fatigue' uses up resources in the women's sector which could be used for other purposes and contributes to a sector feeling that there is a blockage in progressing gender equality issues. This may have the longer-term effect of discouraging participation in these processes.

Conclusions

Formal electoral politics in Northern Ireland is a heavily masculinised domain, in terms of the gendered bodies in political spaces, how politics operates and the issues it prioritises. Ensuring substantive representation for gender issues is both a process of ensuring that women are included in policy making forums (either as elected representatives and/or gender experts) and challenging ideas of how gender equality is defined by non-feminist actors in a conservative gender order. Within this context, the women's sector, in conjunction with feminist activists in Northern Ireland, has combined to create a wealth of evidence and recommendations for improving gender inequality in the region. This body of evidence, the integration of women's groups into communities and their commitment to putting this evidence forward to government has meant they have become trusted sources of consultation and information in policy making processes relating to gender. However, outside of issues which are predominantly associated with gender there continues to remain a barrier to inclusion and legitimacy. As issues such as peacebuilding, policing, culture and tradition, and more recently Brexit and the COVID-19 pandemic are high on the political agenda and often securitised issues, it is imperative that gendered perspectives are both included and heard in these forums.

Within the policy making environment, there continues to be a need for a greater understanding of what gender equality means and could look like in practice. Whilst ideas of liberal feminist equality may not meet much resistance, this approach only goes so far in practice, for example, quotas to increase women in the NI Assembly have never had traction. However, beyond this, formal approaches which view equality as a means of ensuring complete parity in treatment between men and women ignore and invisiblise the historical and contemporary political and social situation of male dominance. Approaches which do not situate inequality within social and political structures will predominantly only work to improve the lives of certain women and ignore intersecting factors of oppression including but not limited to class, race, sexuality and disability.

Policy making in Northern Ireland, whilst encouraging participation from citizens, can often be stagnant with a zero-sum game approach to rights and resources. Within this environment, movement forward can be slow and at times intransient. With the constant rounds of crisis in governance, this can result in periods of intense rounds of consultation on particular issues but if these aren't then moved forward and translated into tangible policies with outcomes, this becomes a cycle of evidence production, writing and submission with no end result. In this way, while feminist actors may try to shape formal political processes in Northern Ireland, the lack of tangible results can breed frustration and a lack of trust in the policy process.

Notes

1 For a discussion of the legal ambiguity around enforceability of Section 75 of the NIA please see McLaughlin and Farris (2004) The Section 75 Equality Duty – An Operational Review. NIO. Available at https://orca.cardiff.ac.uk/id/eprint/58386/1/NORTHERN_IRELAND_OFFICE_2004%5E%5E%5E.pdf (last accessed 02/12/2023).
2 Women's Aid NI (October 2023) Response to the Strategic Framework. Available at https://www.womensaidni.org/assets/uploads/2023/11/Womens-Aid-Federation-NI-WAFN-Response-to-EVAWG-Strategy-Consultation-FINAL.pdf (last accessed 02/12/2023).

3 NICVA State of the Sector: https://www.nicva.org/stateofthesector (last accessed 03/12/2023).
4 Find the Feminist COVID 19 Recovery Plan here: https://wrda.net/wp-content/uploads/2021/07/WPG-COVID-19-Feminist-Recovery-Plan-Relaunch-One-Year-On.pdf (last accessed 02/12/2023).
5 Interview 14, 2022.
6 The Commission's recommendations can be found here: https://www.executiveoffice-ni.gov.uk/sites/default/files/publications/execoffice/commission-on-fict-final-report.pdf (last accessed 03/12/2023).
7 Interview 2, 2012 reported in Pierson, C. (2015) Gender security: Women's experiences of (in)security and policing in post-agreement Northern Ireland. Unpublished PhD Thesis, Ulster University.
8 Interview 5, 2022.
9 Interview 15, 2022.
10 Interview 25, 2022.
11 Focus Group 1, 2012.
12 Interview 7, 2022.
13 STEM stands for Science, Engineering, Technology and Mathematics. Professions which are male-dominated.
14 Interview 8, 2022.
15 Interview 11, 2022.
16 Interview 14, 2022.

4

Women, peace and security? Gender-based violence, legacies of conflict and masculinities

An end to conflict following a peace agreement is often presented as an end to violence. Peace processes prioritise a return to 'normality', an end to public violence and the rebuilding and transfer of power back to the state and its institutions. The aftermath of conflict can also mean a return to traditional and often conservative gender roles (Meintjes et al., 2001). Once violent conflict has ceased, systematic violence is deemed to have ended and consequent analysis views violence as limited to isolated incidents. Whilst peacebuilding processes have shifted to a human security and human rights–based approach, prioritizing the security of the individual or the community, the humans prioritised in these approaches are often framed in a gender-neutral manner (Hudson, 2005). The disproportionate effects of conflict on women is now well-established and gender-based violence in conflict is now an internationally recognized phenomenon. The development of international policy including UN Security Council 1325 on Women, Peace and Security (WPS) has, however, conceptualised this violence through a focus on widespread and systemic rape strategically used in war which has continued to render invisible other gender-based harms and violence such as intimate partner violence and sexual harassment (Kelly, 2000). There is evidence to suggest that certain forms of gender-based violence rise after war or conflict in tandem with the reintegration of male combatants into society. Rises in domestic and intimate partner violence have been observed in conflicts globally and point to limited understandings of an end to violence.

Feminists in post-conflict transitions ask the important question, an end to violence for who? Explorations of violence have led to several feminist scholars developing a theory of continuums. Continuums theory emphasises the connections between forms of violence and suggests distinctions are socially and legally constructed. Liz Kelly has developed the notion of a 'continuum of sexual violence' which aims to broaden legal definitions of violence by highlighting that violence in the private and public sphere are not mutually exclusive (Kelly, 2013). Such distinctions, often made by law, create a hierarchy of violence and make certain types of violence less visible.

Caroline Moser rejects definitions of violence as interpersonal or social and develops a framework which presents a continuum of political, social and economic violence with important linkages between types (Moser, 2001). This holistic view of violence is based on notions of gendered power which reinforce male dominance. Using Galtung's theory of structural violence Cynthia Cockburn reasons that 'the power imbalance of gender relations … are like a linking thread, a kind of fuse, along which violence runs' (Cockburn, 2001: 22, also Cockburn 2010). Cockburn names this the 'gendered continuum of violence' which transcends categories and links forms of violence which arise at different points during conflict.

The importance of viewing gender-based violence through the lens of continuums theory is highlighted in societies coming out of violent conflict. Since the agreement recorded rates of domestic and sexual violence have risen year on year in Northern Ireland (Pierson, 2019). This violence is divorced from the violence of the conflict and the militarised masculine identities it nurtured. Categories of violence create hierarchies that distinguish certain types of violence as being more relevant to peacebuilding. In Northern Ireland, it has been noted that domestic violence was not deemed worthy of extensive political discussion during the peace process essentially designating it to be a 'private' matter. Defining what is called violence is a political decision and creating hierarchies of ordinary and extraordinary violence heightens the invisibility of what is perceived as non-conflict related violence. Whilst feminist academics have attempted to uncover histories of gender-based violence in Northern Ireland there is limited recognition of this violence in memory and legacy work. Understanding historical legacies of gender-based violence is important in addressing such violence in the present both in terms of understanding dominant framings of masculinity which normalise violence and in ongoing legacies of conflict and gender-based violence. This chapter argues that there is a continued silence around gender-based violence which is difficult to break but continues to impact access to justice and to shape contemporary masculinities. Whilst there has been work on bringing a gendered or feminist perspective to peacebuilding in NI focusing heavily on the WPS agenda, this focuses much more substantively on participation than on violence. I demonstrate here that in order to address gender-based violence in the present we must take account of violence in the past and its continuing impact on contemporary masculinities and justice.

Gender-based violence, conflict and masculinities

That war and conflict are gendered experiences with disproportionate impacts on women has only relatively recently been recognised in academic and policy making spheres. Yet the multifaceted nature of harms that women experience in conflict has largely been flattened into recognition of sexual violence. This of course does not capture the full spectrum of harms against women in the public and private sphere. In many ways, gender-based violence in conflict is a layering on of violence, an exacerbation of violences which exist outside of conflict but which can become systemic and intensified (Ní Aoláin et al., 2011). Violences seen and recognised within conflict impacts on what is included within peace negotiations and agreements and accountability in terms of access to justice and reparations.

The recognition of sexual violence in conflict has gone from explanations of it as an opportunistic crime borne from a breakdown in law and order to its codification as a war crime and a serious violation of international humanitarian law. The visible and systemic nature of sexual violence in conflicts such as Rwanda and the former Yugoslavia in the early 1990s and some successful prosecutions in the International Tribunals arising in the aftermath of these conflicts contributed to this recognition. Feminist theorists of war and conflict explained such violence as a weapon of war, a means to emasculate the enemy and further to this a means of ethnic cleansing in situations of enforced pregnancy. The public, systemic and extreme nature of such violences means, however, that other violences against women have often become invisible in the international policy making spheres.

Intimate partner violence (IPV) has remained marginal within discussions of gender-based violence in conflict. It is often accepted as a cultural norm and sometimes supported by legal and judicial systems. Research about the association between political violence and intimate partner violence has mainly been of military personnel. It is estimated that perpetration of physical intimate partner violence is up to three times higher for veterans and active-duty servicemen than for the general population (Kwan et al., 2020). Results of studies undertaken in Sri Lanka, Afghanistan, Lebanon and Palestine has shown that exposure to violent conflict was associated with intimate partner violence and other forms of domestic violence. IPV in Sierra Leone and Liberia was influenced by cultural and financial factors, some of which shifted during wartime, women's financial dependence, traditional gender expectations, and social changes that took place during and after the wars in those countries (Horn et al., 2016). Explanations of IPV have been linked to the use of violence to reassert men's socially established position of power in the family or the exacerbation of pre-existing gender inequalities in conflict.

The point when conflict ends and post-conflict begins becomes a much more nebulous distinction when we consider gender-based violence. It is often ignored that for certain groups the post-conflict environment does not offer a reduction in violence. As Fitzsimmons observes 'for many women, the end of war does not mean the advent of security' (Fitzsimmons, 2005: 187). Between war and peace there may often be very little difference for women, in fact security may decrease. The work of Sheila Meintjes in 'The Aftermath' has been influential in documenting how insecurity for women often rises after conflict (Meintjes et al., 2001). Feminist research has supported the claims that in certain situations after conflict, in the instability of transition, it is more likely that trafficking in women will become established, for women to be forced into sex work through economic necessity, for domestic violence to increase, for honour killings to occur and for rape to be prevalent (Giles and Hyndman, 2004). Many researchers on post-conflict societies have observed a marked rise in the violence which women experience post-conflict or that this may be an increase in reporting of such violence. For example, in Côte d'Ivoire, IPV was the most frequently reported form of violence following the period of armed conflict (20.9 per cent among women; 9.9 per cent among men) (Shuman et al., 2016).

Gender-based violence (GBV) is directly linked to unequal gender relations in a particular society and certain forms of masculinity which are prevalent in that society. Masculinity, as a social construct which in dominant forms has a connection to power, dominance and violence, helps to explain and interrogate gender-based violence as it recognises that whilst masculinities are primarily performed by men, it is not only men who perform masculinity (Peretz and Vidmar, 2021). These socially constructed roles shape men's behaviour and personalities and it has been argued that gendered violence is not an aberration but a core function of this form of masculinity (Brownmiller, 1975). Whilst much of the literature focuses on women as victims of GBV, it will also be directed against LGBT+ populations for their perceived transgressions of gender roles and sexuality, and against other men. As we know, gender roles are not monolithic or static but open to shifts and transformations, as such, examining masculinities in transitions from violent conflict can help us to understand trends in gender-based violence.

In conflict, masculinity has been integrally linked to militarisation. Militarisation is complex and pervasive process whereby the provision of security within a society will become increasingly dependent on and connected to the military or a militaristic style of policing (Enloe, 2000). Militarisation is often justified as a means of attaining and maintaining national security and works to normalise or naturalise a resort to violence in the pursuit of security. Enloe's conceptualisation of militarisation strongly criticises the notion that increased military power and spending will lead to increased security and in fact posits the opposite view that militarisation leads to increased insecurity within a particular state and an increased likelihood of intra- or inter-state violence (Enloe, 2002).

Increasingly, it is recognised that there is a functional relationship between masculinity and militarisation (Enloe, 2000). Essential components of a militarised society including aggression, courage and power are also those associated with hegemonic constructions and performances of masculinity. Militarised societies also enforce conservative roles and gender stereotypes onto women (Elshtain, 1987). This enhances male authority over women and posits men in the role of 'protector' and women as the 'protected'. These conceptions of gender can also act to exploit masculinity and use the protection of women to promote war (Elshtain, 1987). As such, social constructions of gender identity can be viewed as a key factor in determining insecurity within a society, in particular for women, as violence is a key mechanism for reinforcing and maintaining a gender order of male supremacy (Caprioli, 2005). Feminist academic critique has underlined the insecurity and inequality which becomes structurally embedded through militarisation and the effects this has for women both in the public and private sphere (Enloe, 2000).

Post-conflict processes can emulate these structures of masculinity, with these environments being 'vividly about male power systems, struggles and identity formation' (Cockburn, 1998: 131). Struggles for power in post-conflict political and peacebuilding processes can reinforce male dominance and certain dominant forms of masculinity. Paying attention to masculinities in societies emerging from violent conflict and how they transform or reformulate is important in addressing both processes of peace and how women experience post-conflict societies. Societies transitioning from conflict must undergo a process of demilitarisation. In the narrowest sense this will include the disarmament and reintegration of combatants (Woodhouse and Ramsbotham, 2000). However, just as important but much less likely to happen, is the challenge to dominant constructions of masculinity which are infused with militarised notions of protection and security during conflict. It is somehow assumed that militarised masculinities will naturally transform in a new environment with little account of how deeply embedded and socialised gender relations are and how peace processes and post-conflict peacebuilding may actually serve to entrench these gender orders.

One of the most well-known policy ecosystems for addressing the differential impact of conflict on men and women and for engaging women in post-conflict peace processes is the UN Security Council suite of resolutions on Women, Peace and Security (WPS). The UN passed Resolution 1325 in October 2000 after the first open session of the Security Council dedicated to women, peace and security. The session was initiated after intensive lobbying by women concerned at the neglect of women's positioning and rights during and after conflict internationally and regionally (Cockburn, 2007). The Resolution acknowledges the specific impact of armed conflict on women and on women's role in preventing and resolving conflict. The UN has passed subsequent Resolutions on the WPS theme, creating a framework which highlights gendered security concerns in conflict including sexual violence, political participation and the role of women in countering violent extremism. The WPS resolutions have been described as a 'bundle of norms' (True and Wiener, 2019) for realising a gender-equal vision of peace and security and the explicit focus on women has powerful potential to highlight the importance, and further the inclusion, of the various lived experiences of women and girls during and after conflict (Hoewer, 2013) and has the potential to disrupt gender norms and push gendered concerns higher up the political agenda (Tryggestad, 2009).

However feminist critique of WPS highlights that the agenda rests on realist assumptions of both 'gender' and 'war' which do not challenge traditional notions of either of these concepts. It is argued that the WPS Resolutions continue to construct violent conflict as inevitable and ultimately aim to make war safer for women rather than prevent war occurring (Cockburn, 2010; Nikoghosyan, 2018). The language used in the Resolutions is important. It can both shape understandings of women's potential contribution to peacebuilding and the issues which are considered integral to gendered peacebuilding. Analysis of the language of the Resolutions has highlighted its presentation of women and men within traditional gender roles and a fixed binary/dualistic relationship (Pratt and Richter-Devroe, 2011). Narrow constructions of femininity and masculinity allow women and men agency but only within certain boundaries and this leads to definite interpretations of how peace and security are to be implemented and by whom. However, more recent Resolutions have begun to reverse this tendency and emphasised women's agency (Martín de la Rosa and Lázaro, 2019).

The key roles ascribed to women through the Resolutions are those of peacebuilder, peacekeeper or victim. This language relies on the feminisation of peace and the assumption that women are naturally weak and vulnerable during conflict (Otto, 2006). Reading between the lines of the text, men are absent from the WPS agenda (Puechguirbal, 2010), with men and boys only being referenced in three Resolutions explicitly (Wright, 2020). The Resolutions may also be described as heteronormative, with little recognition that lesbian, gay, bisexual, transgender, queer or questioning and intersex individuals face homophobic and transphobic violence in conflicted societies. There has been some recognition in WPS forums, although not formally within the Resolutions themselves. At the Security Council debate marking fifteen years of WPS, the non-governmental organisation (NGO) Working Group on WPS did make explicit reference to sexual and gender-based violence against LGBT+ individuals in Iraq (Hagen, 2016). Lack of consideration of gendered power relations creates a false dualism between men and women, where women are implied to be naturally peaceful and in need of protection and men are those creating the violence and discrimination from which women need to be protected. It is also clear by their absence that men are assumed to be those holding the power to grant women's participation and security. Masculinities are also missing from the WPS agenda. Feminist activists and academics have argued that dominant, conservative understandings of masculinities and femininities sustain militarism and normalize and legitimize militarism and war (Cohn, 1987). Transformation of gender orders can be a route to conflict prevention and gender equality.

Sexual violence has been a priority issue on the WPS agenda from its inception. Resolution 1325 recognizes that women are targeted for sexual violence and requires member states and all those involved in peace activities to protect women from sexual violence and to prosecute those responsible for crimes. Subsequent resolutions focused on sexual violence as a security issue. For example, in Resolutions 1820 and 1888, the Security Council acknowledged that sexual violence can be strategically used as a weapon of war in armed conflict as a means to humiliate and dominate members of a community or ethnic group. Whilst the WPS resolutions can be credited with mainstreaming recognition of gender-based violence during conflict it has been argued that this has narrowed its focus to addressing sexual violence as a weapon of war instead of the myriad gender harms (Aroussi, 2017). This emphasis on sexual violence and in particular mass and systemic violence encourages the divisions and binaries of public/private violence and extraordinary/ordinary violence. These divisions render other gendered harms invisible and prioritise victims and survivors of certain types of violence over others. The framing of sexual violence as a security issue also minimises the role of gender inequality and gender orders in these actions, ignoring feminist calls to tackle the role of gender in gender-based violence.

Gender based violence before and after the Agreement

Within the global literature on conflict related violence against women, Northern Ireland remains conspicuous by its absence. This absence has been explained due to the unseen and non-systemic nature of this violence and the location of Northern Ireland within a Western democratic state (Swaine, 2023). However, with regard to domestic violence there is a wide range of evidence which suggests that conflict 'influenced either their relationship to the nature of the violence (women respondents) experienced, their use of the police, police procedures, and police attitudes' (Montgomery and Bell, 1986: 87).

Monica McWilliams body of work documenting domestic violence in Northern Ireland provides valuable insights into the relationship between GBV and the conflict. Statistics on domestic violence were not collected before 2004, however, the lack of contact and trust within many communities towards the police means figures would not have been representative of a true picture. Figures for non-conflict related homicides between 1991 and 1994 reveal that at least 25 per cent of these murders were related to domestic violence with the majority of victims being married to members of the security forces (McWilliams and Spence, 1996). McWilliams work highlights the highly militarized and national security-oriented police force, the use of (both legally and illegally held) weapons in situations of domestic violence, the lack of contact with the police and their response in communities considered 'suspect', the intervention of paramilitaries and the fact of paramilitaries (and members of the security forces) being perpetrators of domestic abuse being significant conflict related factors (McWilliams and Ní Aoláin, 2013). There were a number of firearm certificates being withdrawn annually as legally held 'personal protection weapons' as they had been used in domestic violence situations (McKay, 1985). One of the results was a requirement for police officers to keep their weapons at work. It is clear that conflict had effects on the severity and ability to access justice in situations of intimate partner violence.

Accounting for sexual violence during the conflict has been even more difficult. There is no evidence of mass and systemic sexual violence that has been witnessed in other recent conflicts and human rights bodies reporting during the period of conflict ignored sexual violence apart from the treatment of women in detention. State perpetrated sexual violence used by soldiers, police and prison guards, included invasive body searches, sexual harassment and sexual threats happening at checkpoints and security barriers or searches of homes or when women were held in detention (O'Keefe, 2021; Pickering, 2001). The strip-searching of women prisoners was widely publicized and was reported by Amnesty International as a deliberate attempt to degrade and humiliate women. It is clear that women detained by the state were subjected to a particular form of gendered violence and threat. McWilliams and Ní Aoláin (2013) note the number of rape and sexual assaults which involved guns in the past and present. In 2006, the Belfast Rape Crisis and Sexual Abuse Centre (RCSAC) reported a significantly higher proportion of rapes committed at gunpoint in Northern Ireland, compared to the rest of the UK and Ireland (McWilliams and Ní Aoláin, 2013).

In terms of violence perpetrated by non-state actors, usually paramilitaries, there is evidence of isolated and individual instances, for example, there are reports of gang rapes in Northern Ireland, where a woman's religion has been a factor in the sexual assault (Swaine, 2023). However, the majority of claims which have been emerging, primarily through the media, are those which took place within communities, one of the most well-known of these being the case of Máiría Cahill who is from a prominent Republican family, and alleges she had been raped by an IRA member between 1997 and 1998 and was subjected to a kangaroo court[1] when she reported abuse to senior IRA members. Within the media there have been allegations of a number of sexual assaults carried out by members of paramilitary groups (both Republican and Loyalist), and that many of these crimes have been covered up by members of the same groups (O'Rourke and Swaine, 2017). There are also many people coming forward who had been children at the time of their assault. Within Republican communities, women and girls who had relationships with British soldiers were routinely subject to tarring and feathering as a means of public shaming (Harkin and Kilmurray, 1985). There is an account of Loyalist paramilitaries raping a Catholic woman and of attacking a Nationalist MP's wife and scoring the word UVF into her breasts (reported in Swaine, 2023). Whilst some of these crimes could be labelled as unrelated to conflict, it is clear that many crimes and their cover up were facilitated by the status of perpetrators and the lack of attention given to non-conflict related crime. Swaines (2023) typology of gender-based violence in the Northern Ireland conflict also includes the important classification of reproductive violences which she defines in the context of detention as prevention of access to menstrual products, detention of children with mothers and threats to inform partners of sexual promiscuity.

It has been put forward that the silence around GBV comes from the stigma associated with such crimes (O'Keeffe, 2017) or the lack of status given to gender as a factor in shaping experiences of conflict or in determining victimhood (O'Rourke and Swaine, 2017). Whilst these are convincing arguments, McWilliams and Ní Aoláin (2013: 71) make a pertinent point that 'the political costs of naming prominent men as wife-beaters or rapists when such individuals are lauded as local heroes can compound the vulnerability of their attached women'. It is worth considering that perhaps the majority of GBV during the Troubles period occurred within rather than between communities. This has repercussions at both the structural and individual level. For the individual victim/survivor, naming a perpetrator could also mean naming a member of your own community group, this could mean going against the official community narrative of the perpetrator, troubling community narratives of local heroes as McWilliams and Ní Aoláin (2013) point out and resulting in further vulnerability. At the structural/official level, recognizing GBV means opening up the label of victim to a much larger body of people and therefore the potential for reparations. Gender based violence also troubles many of the distinctions and hierarchies which have been made over the term victim (Jankowitz, 2018), largely the politicised distinction of 'innocent' and 'non-innocent' victims. For example, if a person with no state security or paramilitary connections was harmed in the conflict they are labelled by some groups as an 'innocent victim', if it is discovered that the same person carried out gender-based violence how can the label of 'innocent' still stand?

Gender-based violence in the past appears to be coming into the public domain on an individualized and case-by-case basis through media accounts. There appears to be little political will to document cases in a systematic manner or to recognize officially that such crimes took place and are part of a gendered narrative of the conflict. This continues a narrative which privileges violence which takes place in the public sphere and is directly connected to national security. Official documents that are part of the architecture of peace have a limited understanding of gender. By the same token they make no mention of GBV in the past or present. As Teresa O'Keefe (2017: 75) notes with regard to victims and survivors groups 'the Commission for Victims and Survivors or victim's advocacy groups like Relatives for Justice, Wave or the Pat Finucane Centre, have also not addressed the issue of sexual violence in a meaningful way'. I have noted in a previous publication that I have attended workshops by international organisations who have attempted to begin a conversation on documenting sexual violence within the Northern Ireland conflict but whose work remains out of the public domain due to the difficulty of engaging survivors (Pierson, 2018b). Recent initiatives to begin conceptualizing a gendered perspective on the past still do not reflect on the potential for dealing with GBV, for example the Legacy Gender Integration Group (a group of academics and representatives from victim/survivor groups and human rights NGO's) who developed Gender Principles for Dealing with the Legacy of the Past in 2015 makes no mention of such violence in their report or recommendations (Ahmed et al., 2016).

Recorded rates of GBV in the period since the Agreement highlight how narrow the idea of ending violence through a peace agreement is. Violence is not defined for women solely through conflict or a lack of conflict. Although there may be a reduction in public and political violence after the signing of a peace Agreement, violence in private or against the person may increase (Pillay, 2001). The distinction between 'ordinary' and 'extraordinary' violence or public and private violence persists and creates a dichotomy where certain types of violence can be ignored as unrelated to conflict and therefore peacebuilding. Domestic violence statistics began to be recorded in NI in 2004, since this period PSNI records show that rates of reporting have risen year on year. Between October 2022 and September 2023, 33,229 domestic abuse incidents were reported to the PSNI indicating an increase of 126 (0.4 per cent) on the previous twelve months.[2] Numbers of reports of sexual offences have also increased year on year with approximately 4,232 sexual offences recorded by the PSNI in the 2022–2023 time period.[3] It is difficult to know if GBV is increasing or if there is increased confidence in reporting to the police. However, evidence consistently suggests that GBV crimes are under-reported.

Legacies of the past in the present

Conflict shapes how GBV is experienced and how justice is sought. Similarly, in post-conflict situations, whilst improvements will be made, often for those who live in areas which were most affected by the conflict there will be legacies of conflict which will continue to affect gender justice. However, there is evidence of positive developments in the policing of domestic violence. Doyle and McWilliams (2020) research points to a significant increase in positive appraisals of police response to domestic violence between 1992 and 2016, there is also evidence that there is less likelihood of women reporting domestic abuse to paramilitaries or of abusers claiming paramilitary status to threaten women, however this does still exist on a smaller scale. Swaine (2015) also points to increased numbers of reporting in Nationalist/Republican communities as an indicator of increased confidence in communities which in the past would have been disengaged with policing.

Translating reporting of GBV into tangible outcomes for victims/survivors remains an issue. Northern Ireland has a lower rate of convictions for sexual violence than the rest of the UK. The conviction rate for rape is 1.8 per cent in Northern Ireland, compared to 3.3 per cent in England and Wales and 5.2 per cent in Scotland (Killean et al., 2021). An independent review of the law and procedure relating to serious sexual offence cases in Northern Ireland was undertaken in 2018 (Gillen, 2019). The sixteen recommendations made in the report to improve the current system have received little progression due to lack of a functioning Executive and lack of budgetary commitment (Killean et al., 2021).

GBV as an issue of peace and security remains peripheral to NI discussions. This divorces contemporary aspects of GBV from their link to ongoing legacies of conflict and particular aspects of control within communities. As noted above, paramilitary groups have been responsible for GBV both within their own communities and against other communities. Paramilitary control over some communities is ongoing twenty-five years after the Agreement and policies such as The Tackling Paramilitarism Programme is designed to support the transition of paramilitary groups toward community-development, restorative justice, and conflict-transformation practices.

The only reference to women in this programme is a Developing Women in Community Leadership Programme which will provide women with the skills, knowledge and confidence they need to become influencers and take on roles such as leadership and decision-making in their communities. However, the programme makes no mention of GBV or links between paramilitarism and GBV.

Analysis of WPS from a feminist perspective has highlighted paramilitary control and women's participation in peacebuilding and community politics (Pierson, 2019; Turner and Swaine, 2021), however, links between GBV and paramilitary control are not as prevalent. In recent research, young women report being victims of ongoing paramilitary violence, with gendered aspects to this violence including the use of sexual violence against women (McAlister et al., 2022). Young men have also been the victims of militarised masculinities where anti-social behaviour was, and in some cases continues to be, heavily policed through informal community justice (Ashe and Harland, 2014). As one participant highlighted, whilst there may be less likelihood of threats of paramilitary power in domestic and sexual abuse this does still occur:

> you still see it used in a way that isn't talked about in mainstream discussions of women, peace and security. You still see it used as a tool of coercive control within communities, and you still see the threat of it used as a tool of attempted control of anybody who would speak out, you know, in any way criticising those controlling entities or the organizations, as the women I work with tend to call them. So you see it both in practice and in the threat of it all the time, and when, interestingly, when we were doing the research that we did on ... violence against women and girls ... a lot of people mentioned exactly that unprompted. They were not asked in any way, but they started talking about how you know this paramilitary control in their area, and people connected with it saying...I'm connected in some way, and therefore through my connection you cannot speak out, and that person doesn't necessarily know if that's true or not, but you also see it used explicitly as a tool. When anytime you speak out and somebody doesn't like what you're saying the violent threats often become sexual.[4]

The policing of GBV also continues to be affected by the aspects of national security and conflict-style policing. The use of informants during the Northern Ireland Troubles and in the post-Agreement period in Republican and Loyalist communities to infiltrate paramilitary organisations is well documented (Moran, 2010). Recruitment of informers was undertaken by the RUC (Special Branch), the Army and MI5. It has been noted that such individuals were often protected from criminal sanction through either official or unofficial sheltering. The most serious allegations against the RUC are of collusion with informers in high profile murders.

Participants in a focus group in a previous piece of research (Pierson, 2015) noted that the recruitment of informers was a widespread phenomenon in their community (a community in Belfast which was, and continues to be, one of the most affected by the conflict) and resulted in very negative experiences of the police for informers (female) partners and women within the community in general. Such negative experiences resulted in cases of domestic abuse where the perpetrator would be sheltered as such abuse is considered of less importance than counter-insurgency police work. In addition, these women felt that many committing crimes in their community were being used as informants, therefore having immunity and lessening confidence in the police for the community as a whole:

> The cops will turn round and say there's no touts (*informants*) but of course there is...there was a wee fella down the road who was always doing burglaries and joy riding and he killed someone and he was charged under section 18 or 20 or something ... the solicitors call it the touts section...and the wee lad just kept getting out and out and out and he was killing people, he was doing anything he wanted because he was giving names over...how are women meant to feel safe with that when the cops are actually working hand in hand with them 'un's. There's good cops and bad cops but at the end of the day there's more bad cops round here than good. Only when they stop working with them to get names, it's always been like that here[5].

The marginalisation of GBV as a part of discussions of the legacies of the conflict of NI has left a gap in understandings of the past which leak tangibly into experiences of GBV and access to justice in the present. Theorising of violence by feminist scholars has developed a continuums approach which challenges understandings of binary approaches to violence as public or private sphere or conflict and non-conflict related violence to illustrate the interlinking nature of all violence. These approaches have also highlighted how a supposed end to political violence in the form of a peace agreement does often not mean a reduction in violence for everyone, in particular women. Continuums are even more explicit when looked at through the lens of the conflict/post-conflict binary and how past narratives of security and justice manifest in the present. Without interrogation of broader forms of violence in the past, how these impact justice in the present remains silenced.

Contemporary masculinities in local and global context

The dynamics of conflict and subsequent peacebuilding shape gender norms and behaviours. Conflict has been specifically linked to what are termed 'hyper' forms of masculinity which describe 'a masculinity in which the strictures against femininity and homosexuality are especially intense and in which physical strength and aggressiveness are paramount' (Caprioli and Boyer, 2001: 78). This form of masculinity has particular social and political traction and will affect how women experience violence. Specific hyper-masculine manifestations of masculinity were observed in NI, related to ethno-national identity and political violence, with feminists aptly describing the region during conflict as an 'armed patriarchy' (Edgerton, 1986: 76). As noted above, processes of demilitarisation in societies emerging from violent conflict rarely take the transformation of militarised masculinities into account, in fact, peace and security are often assumed to depend on a return to a traditional gender order with men in positions of power in the public and private sphere. This has been referred to as 'masculinity nostalgia' and a yearning for patriarchal gender orders (MacKenzie and Foster, 2017). Here, I wish to argue that this nostalgia is both localised and globalised with some nostalgia for militarised masculinities happening in tandem with a global backlash on women's rights which is conceptualised through nostalgia for conservative gender orders and 'family values'.

In Northern Ireland, legal processes of demilitarisation were followed, however, the process of demilitarisation in Northern Ireland has been judged to be narrow (even in mainstream terms) focussing on the decommissioning of paramilitary weapons (Smyth, 2004). The legacy of militarisation and its continued effects on gender roles, power and control within communities, and the provision of security remain under analysed. Whilst men are often the subject of research and analysis, their gendered identities remain peripheral (Ashe, 2012). As noted in Chapter 1, there were a range of options for men to protect their nation and community, via adopting militarised masculinities through formal security services or paramilitary organisations. In the transitional period, men's control of communities continues through peacebuilding work and both informal and formal community justice. As a participant in a previous research project told me about discussing issues of peace and security 'women are afraid … we had a meeting and explained how important it was for women to leave their own communities to have those conversations on difficult issues'.[6] In this way, there is a continued legitimisation of militarised masculinities as both leaders of and protectors of communities and fear from those men of women's organising.

However, nostalgia for gender roles in conflict may not only be experienced by men. As theorised by feminists, conflict can open up space for women to move into the public sphere. Perceptions of women being non-violent actors can mean that they can move in public spaces more easily than men and in some circumstances can feel safer. As one participant explained in a previous piece of research on gender security:

women have had a lot more flexibility because, in terms of their personal safety during the conflict and afterwards, because they weren't men, you know they weren't picked up, beat up, all the things that happened and we all know the stories that women could escort men home because if you were seen with a woman you were less likely to be picked up.[7]

The same participant explained that she didn't feel this safety any longer and would be unlikely to walk around at night alone. Similar sentiments were expressed to me by other participants and exemplify the complexity of transitions from militarised security frameworks which must be accompanied by transitions in gender orders which enable women to feel safe from violence.

Ideals of masculinity can also be embedded through cultural landscapes where militarised masculinities are commemorated and used as a tool to build a collective national identity through 'masculinized memory, masculinized humiliation and masculinized hope' (Enloe, 1990: 45). Even when women are included in commemoration activity, this is often highly gendered and tokenistic (McDowell, 2008). Memory work in Northern Ireland is a means of (often competing) representation and interpretation of experiences of the Troubles for communities but layered onto this they are representations of gendered narratives. Visual representations of conflict in the form of murals have been described by McDowell (2008: 340) as 'reproducing and reinforcing masculinity' with a heavy focus on male paramilitary actors. Continuing to privilege and uphold this identity through commemoration, maintains its power and as such it becomes a draw to younger men (and on occasion women) who wish to gain status and control within their community. Violent expressions of masculinity in younger men have been described in part through the maintenance of ethnic power but also as a response to the social marginalisation of those men through educational underachievement and a lack of employment.

Masculinities whilst being contextual also link to global trends. Currently, we are witnessing a backlash in women's rights and a rise in anti-gender politics. This backlash can be seen at both international levels such as the UN and its blocking of sexual and reproductive rights in the UN WPS agenda (Thomson and Pierson, 2018) and in national regressions such as rescindments of abortion rights in the United States and anti-trans rights politics in Britain. Movements to regress gender rights are highly coordinated and have backing from global religious and civil society organisations and certain states such as the United States and some post-Soviet states (Cupać and Ebetürk, 2020). They conceptualise their work within the framing of restoring 'family values' and the idea that gender equality has gone too far and that men are now disadvantaged. Alter and Zürn (2020) provides a framework for analysing backlash politics which encompasses three necessary elements, first a retrograde objective of returning to a prior social condition, second, extraordinary goals and tactics that challenge dominant scripts, and third a threshold condition of entering mainstream public discourse.

Retrograde objectives are particularly pertinent when examining masculinities. These are viewed to often generate emotional appeals, including nostalgia and negative sentiments such as anger and resentment (Alter and Zürn, 2020: 566). Previously, in a society such as NI, where conflict had heightened masculine power it could hardly be claimed that 'feminism had gone too far' yet more recently with progressions in gender rights such as abortion and more visibly women in political leadership positions there is more potential for masculine nostalgia. Participants noted that in political forums to discuss gender equality, a lack of understanding of how gendered inequality has historical and contextualised roots meant that there had been a push to make such forums gender equal in terms of representation of women's and men's rights groups despite inequality manifesting much more prominently for women. One participant noted that policymakers think they are starting on a 'blank page' without consideration of the history of male dominance and conservative gender relations which exemplify society and politics in NI.

The backlash against gender rights, its link to extreme misogyny online and the influence of this on young men is now being taken more seriously as an aspect of right-wing extremism (Nicholas, 2024). Explicit misogyny, anti-feminism and masculine aggrievement are key aspects of right-wing extremism and links between IPV and acts of right-wing extremist violence have been found by researchers (Scaptura and Boyle, 2020: 279). However, beyond acts of extreme mass violence are the right-wing personalities' covert ideas of tradition, hierarchy, order and entitlement that also underpin violence-supportive attitudes that are a driver of intimate partner violence (Nicholas, 2024: 2). What has been termed the 'manosphere', a loosely connected group of anti-feminist communities, has effects on men's attitudes towards women and towards violence as an aspect of masculinity which of course have effects in offline spaces. As one participant noted, we cannot treat NI as a place apart with regard to developing global anti-feminist cultures:

> But the other barrier that I think is a bit more scary is the rise of the far right … it's reaching a lot of young men online, its invisible and behind closed doors. But we can start to see more organized violence, misogynist violence, transphobic violence normalized. We are dealing with bunch of lads who literally think that this is fine because they're listening to some podcast. Just last week there was a situation where one of the biggest, transphobic sites on the

Internet was taken down by a couple of trans women here in Belfast, but it was clear from some of the interactions that that site had active members in Belfast. We think we're small and insignificant in relation to those big global movements. But we're not.[8]

The impact of anti-feminist views of women can be exemplified through high-profile incidents such as the Ulster Rugby rape trial. Throughout the 2018 trial of Ulster rugby players accused of rape, evidence from the defendants WhatsApp messages, views expressed by the legal team and in the media made clear that highly regressive views of women and their sexuality persist both in private conversations and public statements and that these views have tangible impacts on violences committed against women and their access to justice.

WPS as a framework for addressing GBV

Policy on GBV has stagnated in NI (Michelle O'Neill, the current First Minister stated in February 2024 that introducing a new framework on violence against women would be a priority for the new Executive). However, a policy which does not take account of the historical legacies of GBV and the impact of gender roles can only tackle part of the problem. One means to open wider conversations is linking GBV to the implementation of WPS.

The use of international frameworks can be viewed as a tool borne from frustration, when issues are being blocked at a local or national level, it may seem that the only option is to move to 'venue shop' and move to a higher authority in order to hold the state accountable for its (in)action. This form of moral leverage (Keck and Sikkink, 1998) helps groups gain more influence than they could on their own and relies on mobilizing shame, assuming states are vulnerable to the opinions of others outside. It also works to blur the boundaries of the state, for example with the WPS agenda, activists in NI have appealed to both Westminster and the Republic of Ireland. In addition to moving a stagnant policy agenda, the use of international norms by activists and civil society has an outward focus and is part of a broader cultural shift. Activists become simultaneously domestic and international actors, creating both formal and informal networks of information, advocacy tools, support and strategy. This is a particularly transnational feminist strategy, recognizing the commonalities of struggle and attempting to globally connect ideas whilst acknowledging difference.

One of the obvious uses of international norms is their invocation of legitimacy. As Cortell and Davis note 'when a norm is salient in a particular social discourse, its invocation by relevant actors legitimates a particular behaviour or action, creating a prima facie obligation, and thereby calling into question or delegitimating alternative choices' (2000: 69). Salience of course is key in this equation, salience may be measured through a norms permeation in national discourse in demands for change and how it is embedded in institutions and policies. One of the processes that activists engage in therefore is norm implementation, they translate international norms for both political actors and the general public, attempting to 'vernaculize' and 'indigenize' them in a way that is resonant (Ferree, 2003). This improves understanding of rights as they become framed in local understandings rather than imposed from above.

Resolution 1325 was passed after the peace negotiations in Northern Ireland that culminated in the 1998 Agreement. The Resolution was, therefore, not integrated into the Agreement, yet it has the potential to impact on gendering peacebuilding in the region through implementation in the future. In terms of National Action Plans both the UK and the Republic of Ireland have WPS NAPs. The UK has recently released its fifth NAP. This is the first time that Northern Ireland has been included, previously international bodies such as the CEDAW Committee have called for the UK to include NI in its NAP in their reviews of the UK. The exclusion of NI was believed to be a lack of willingness of the UK government to define NI as a conflict. The UK's fifth NAP refers to NI in several places. First, the Northern Ireland Office had input into the plan, second, in its domestic implementation section through championing and highlighting expertise from women peacebuilders in Northern Ireland to the governments Preventing Sexual Violence in Conflict Initiative Team of Experts. Third, to recognise and promote the crucial work of Northern Ireland's women in peacebuilding with the 25th Anniversary of the Agreement and finally through the commitment to co-design a Northern Ireland Strategy on Ending Violence Against Women and Girls with stakeholders. All three of the Republic of Ireland's NAPs include Northern Ireland, after intensive lobbying from civil society in both the north and south of Ireland. Importantly the ROI's NAP specifically mentions funding of civil society groups in the promotion of WPS and regular meetings with civil society groups engaged in WPS work.

Locally, the Northern Ireland Assembly has established an All-Party Group on Women, Peace and Security. All Party Groups provide a forum for politicians across the party spectrum and external organisations to share knowledge and discuss issues. Whilst the group is active and has a wide party membership, translating this into tangible policy commitments is more difficult (Thomson, 2017). Within the community and voluntary sector there is a tangible sense of ownership and commitment to the WPS agenda. There are a plethora of grassroots and women's groups' activities to raise awareness of WPS in local communities, lobby for implementation and produce research detailing potential focal points for a Northern Ireland Action Plan (Hinds and Donnelly, 2014; Pierson and Radford, 2016).

Much of the focus on WPS is on women's participation and inclusion of gendered expertise in peacebuilding, gender-based violence has had limited attention compared to other conflicts where GBV has been more widespread and systemic. Therefore, it is positive to see that the UK's most recent action plan includes policy on GBV as part of the remit of WPS and this is a potential inroad to linking contemporary policy on GBV to past legacies of gender-based violence. Whilst feminist research has uncovered and highlighted the continuums of such violence and that they are a legacy issue in the NI context, these understandings remain on the periphery of policy making.

Conclusions

As has been demonstrated throughout this chapter, distinctions of conflict and post-conflict become less relevant when applied to gender-based violence. In many circumstances, rates of GBV rise after conflict and can be linked to ideals of masculinity fostered during conflict yet rarely noted as an aspect of peace agreements or post-conflict peacebuilding. However, they have tangible impacts on experiences of violence and justice in post-conflict environments. Without recognition of these legacies of violence and masculinity and their impact in contemporary instances of violence, it is likely that any policy mechanisms introduced on the theme of GBV will fall short of tackling the root of the problem. As I have suggested here the WPS agenda may be one route to challenging this. Linking policies on GBV to peace and security allows for conversations about the past and the conflation of Northern Ireland as a conflict without such violence. In addition, it can also open up conversations about masculinities, both in the past and the present. With the WPS link to preventing conflict, the legacy of militarised masculinities and new masculinities in the form of extreme misogyny (and its link to the far right) and their influence on gender-based violence can be discussed as an ongoing security concern rather than individualised acts of violence.

Notes

1 An unofficial court where victims are brought into interrogation spaces with the perpetrator.
2 https://www.psni.police.uk/system/files/2024-02/1121995173/Domestic%20Abuse%20Bulletin%20Period%20Ending%2031st%20December%202023.pdf (last accessed 12/02/2025).

3 https://www.statista.com/statistics/941371/sexual-offences-in-northern-ireland/ (last accessed 12/02/2025.
4 Interview 5, 2022.
5 Focus Group 6, 2015.
6 Focus Group 1, 2014.
7 Interview 18, 2014.
8 Interview 9, 2022.

5

Beyond the state: prefigurative politics and abortion care activism

Governance, institutions and politics in Northern Ireland have been often described as being set up to prioritise and reinforce sectarianism and a separation of communities. The political functioning of Northern Ireland is often characterised by periods of crisis and instability. The lack of functioning governance has been referenced as a feature which has contributed to the strength and vibrancy of civil society organising in the region. More recently, it has been argued that the instability that typifies Northern Irish politics in fact has created conditions that mean that feminist and other social movement actors are able to respond to crisis, such as the COVID-19 pandemic, more effectively through collective political strategies formulated in previous periods of crisis (Deiana et al., 2022).

However, political decision-making facilitated on discourses of threat and crisis can be used to protect, save and care for valued lives and damage, destroy and abandon other lives. In this way, the political situation of Northern Ireland sets limitations on who we care for and about. Care is assumed to depend on family relations or community affiliation. Caring is also a highly gendered domain, and as discussed below, the feminisation of care labour has contributed to its devaluation in society. The aim of this chapter is to interrogate abortion care provided outside of the state in activist networks, through the 'unsettledness' of Northern Ireland politics and to argue that the intransigency of, and dissatisfaction with, contemporary political structures can provide spaces from within which more radical political activity can emerge and different political futures can be imagined and enacted in contemporary political practice. In this way, feminist politics is operating at 'the radical in-between of prefigurative politics and the politics of survival' (Lin et al., 2016: 302).

Abortion rights activism in Northern Ireland presents a vital case study in how this prefigurative and survival politics can manifest to produce what prefigurative politics scholars call 'the deliberate experimental implementation of desired future social relations and practices in the here and now' (Raekstad and Gradin, 2020: 10). Whilst abortion was decriminalised in

2019, the commissioning of abortion services by the Department of Health has taken years to secure. Before and after legal change activists have continued with their work providing material support to abortion seekers, attempting to shift mindsets on abortion rights and decentralising the state in abortion care and politics. In this way, abortion politics provides an imaginative political opening to shift our understandings of how care is provided, who we should care about and the role of the state in defining these relationships.

As Vivaldi and Stutzin write 'activism has never flourished in some abstract "ideal" space' (2021: 241), this chapter highlights that in fact imperfect and difficult political spaces have contributed (however unwillingly) to a politics and activism around abortion which provides a scaffold to protect rights against state regressions but also a transformative vision of the future of abortion care. Abortion rights activists are addressing crises that are not highlighted or emphasised by dominant political actors but that have real effects on women's lives and equality. This future vision of abortion care challenges the role of the state and also the boundaries of gender and traditional political communities in terms of questioning who takes part in care work and who we should care about and for. In this way abortion politics can reimagine ideas of both community and care.

The Northern Irish movement connects ongoing contemporary conversations in global abortion rights movements around care activism and recognition the state cannot have complete monopoly and power over abortion as this also gives it the opportunity to regress laws and access. As such, this chapter contributes to a growing global literature on the prefigurative nature of abortion activism and care.

Prefigurative politics and feminist strategy

This chapter situates feminist modes of abortion care as forms of prefigurative politics. The term prefigurative politics emerges from strands of anarchist and Marxist thought with the aim of developing a political praxis where transformative social change happens through the contemporary establishment of the future structures that we wish to see within our current movements and organisations. Effectively, this argues that we cannot use the strategies, institutions and organisations of the present to achieve the social change of the future. At the heart of this is a reflexive consideration of the relationship between present political action and organising, and the future goal of a transformed politics and society (Swain, 2019). Liberation within our social relations will not appear from organisation and practices which emulate current structures – they must be developed deliberately or else we risk ending up reproducing the systems we are attempting to overthrow. Srnicek and Williams (2015) caution however that this potentially purist approach where means must match the ends may become dogmatic perhaps ignoring or minimising structural forces that are set against movements. Similarly, Lugones (2003) argues that movements can't act outside the struggles of everyday life and must be grounded in acting against oppression.

The development of the term prefigurative politics came through the work of Carl Boggs in the 1970s and his work on New Left movements and socialist political strategy. Boggs provides a broad definition of prefigurative politics as an organisation or movement embodying 'those forms of social relations, decision-making, culture and human experience that are its ultimate goal' (Boggs, 1977: 100). Boggs problematises the supposed zero-sum approach to the two arenas of activity for the left. That is that instrumental or strategic politics (the struggle for political power) and prefigurative, (achieving revolutionary goals of self-emancipation and collective social relations) cannot be worked on together as one must take away from the other (Yates, 2021). Prefigurative politics is often critiqued as being naïve, non-strategic or apolitical, whereas instrumental politics is viewed to have more strategic potential. However, Törnberg (2021) suggests that prefigurative strategies do not have to be peripheral or incremental aspects of political and social change but can actually be revolutionary if they are able scale up when opportunity arises for changes in the sociopolitical landscape. A useful example of this idea can be found in abortion politics. The discovery, by Brazilian women in a legally restrictive regime, that misoprostal (an ulcer medication) could be used as an abortifacient has ultimately led to this becoming a standard medication recommended by the WHO for medical abortion and used globally for early medical abortion (Bloomer et al., 2018).

Definitions and typologies of prefigurative politics bring out particularly important and integral aspects to the practice. Raekstad and Gradin (2020) trace the history of prefigurative politics and practices through utopian socialism, anarchism, Marxism and feminism with key themes of prefiguration being the fundamental link between aims and methods of movements, the abolition of hierarchical organising, the establishment of desired practices in the here and now and the importance of everyday practices. Raekstad and Saio Gradin also point to the limitations of the broad definition arguing that activity to be considered prefigurative must be a deliberate implementation of desired future social relations now and that by their nature they will also likely be experimental. This means that there must be an intent to create future structures in the present with the potential for failure. Yates (2021) categorises the functions of prefigurative politics as being

(i) part of a process of substituting or supplanting institutions, (ii) about experimentation, innovation and learning, (iii) preparing or resourcing collective actors, (iv) a way of directly achieving something in the here and now and, (v) a mode of doing activism that pays attention to the micropolitics of political activity. He suggests that the future questions of prefiguration of movement should focus on how prefigurative projects are negotiated within movements, how they are influenced by interactions with opponents and allies and how and where combining strategic elements has been successful (Yates, 2021).

However, a focus on definitions may lose the explanatory potential of prefigurative politics (Jeffrey and Dyson, 2021). It may be more useful to focus on how prefiguration is practised. Jeffrey and Dyson (2021) argue that these practices must involve issues of power, conflict and transformation to qualify as prefigurative. Lin et al. (2016), in their description of Black feminist reproductive justice group BRAVE (Building Reproductive Autonomy and Voices for Equity) in the United States imagine a praxis of prefigurative politics which is based on three premises a) the creation of transformative, relational spaces where values can be shaped – so-called 'radical homeplaces' where community and belonging are developed; b) bids for self-determination derived from lived experience – theory in the flesh and recognition of the importance of body politics; and c) intersectional engagement in coalitions, where such organising is necessary as we cannot be divorced from our experience of overlapping oppressions.

Engaging in prefigurative strategies or modes of organising means that social movement actors must engage in futural thinking with 'the idea that a transformative social movement must necessarily anticipate the ways and means of the hoped-for new society' (Tokar, 2003). This involves thinking about long-term effects of present actions, organising and structures, and as noted above will inevitably involve experimental and untested strategies. However, at present, looking towards the future with climate change, rising inequality and conflict may look bleak (Gordon, 2018). Engaging in prefigurative politics may involve more of a radical hope or a sense that there is no need for a distinct vision of how a future society will look or function but that acting in anti-authoritarian or non-hierarchical ways is enough (Gordon, 2018; Graeber, 2002). As Maeckelbergh argues, prefiguration is something that is done rather than theorised (2011).

Prefigurative strategies are closely related to feminist political movements. However, this is not to say that patriarchal structures will necessarily be resolved within revolutionary movements. Prefigurative politics can have potential for feminism within movements also. Feminist politics in broader social movements such as socialist or emancipatory nationalist movements have often seen what Rowbotham (1985) referred to as the politics of deferment – where questions such as 'the woman question' are viewed by leaders (often male) to be able to be deferred until after the revolution. In regions affected by conflict and within national liberation movements, feminists have theorised an opening of space for women to move into the public sphere and take on positions of leadership, yet also recognise that this space closes in the aftermath of conflict with the assumption that with the reintegration of men, women will simply move back into the private sphere (Meintjes et al., 2001). Prefigurative strategies question the assumption that women's liberation can wait as the current implementation of future social relations are imperative to the political project and organising.

Stall and Stoeker's (1998) analysis of community organising in the United States illustrates how gender structures provide very different experiences of social movement organising for men and women. Contrasting the approach of Saul Alinsky (a community organiser and political theorist) with women centred models of community organising they illustrate how Alinsky's model, with its focus on building power in the public sphere and a masculinist mode of organising and leadership replicates a zero-sum game approach to power similar to that seen in the electoral political domain. Women centred organising, they argue, views power as limitless and collective and does not rely on sole, charismatic leaders for its continuance. This method of organising has more potential to challenge power relations and the public/private divide in politics but may have less traction and voice in connecting with formal politics. As such women-centred organising may be viewed as prefigurative but less strategic.

It is not only organisations that can practice prefigurative politics but broader culture, social relations and everyday practice. This of course draws on some of the core tenets of feminist organising and thought, that the personal is political. How people organize, the knowledge they prioritize, who leads, can all serve to legitimise new hierarchies and modes of domination and simply put new faces into old institutions. Bell hooks (2013) critique of Sheryl Sandbergs book 'Lean In' explains this clearly, hooks argues that Sandbergs book which advocates for gender equality within the existing system through 'leaning in' and aiming to have more women head businesses as a faux feminism which does nothing to challenge existing patriarchal structures and sees gender inequality primarily as a problem which can be fixed. Her book also relies on a 'trickle down' version of feminism which assumes that more women at the top will be better for all women. This type of thinking does little to challenge patriarchal thinking and structures.

Feminist political projects have long been explicitly prefigurative. The Combahee River Collective statement in 1977 is an often-cited example of this. The US Black feminist lesbian group based in Boston practiced revolutionary socialist politics including educational work, consciousness-raising groups, supporting those targeted by the police. Their statement is well-known as being the first use of the term 'identity politics', referencing the fact that as Black lesbian women they often did not feel their interests included by broader (white) feminist movements and did not need to be liberated by such groups. This statement of intersectional oppression highlights that the radical restructuring of society that needs to be done in order to address intersecting inequalities must be done by a broad range of people with reference to our personal experiences and identities. More recently, this form of intersectional prefiguration has been highlighted in terms of internal movement politics and praxis with the example of the UK based anti-austerity group Sisters Uncut who campaign on the gendered and intersectional aspects of the UK's austerity policies (Ishkanian and Peña Saavedra, 2019). They argue that challenging hierarchies and privileges in the group are seen as equally if not more important than achieving wider political and policy goals. The work of interrogating gender, class and inclusion within a movement is not easy and is an ongoing, messy and complex praxis. It has resulted in difficult moments but Sisters Uncut have developed sessions on learning and reflecting within movements and an Accountability Toolkit, emphasising ongoing reflective feminism and prefigurative practice.

Early work on prefigurative politics included the state, governments and parties alongside social movements in their definition of collectives undertaking prefigurative strategies but this trend was reversed in the 1990s and currently prefigurative strategies are positioned primarily as a feature of social movements (Yates, 2021). Feminist prefigurative politics brings into question the relationship between feminism and the state. There has been a distinct push over the past fifteen years for states to adopt policies which appear to focus on gender equality, as detailed earlier in this text, the development and implementation of the UN Women, Peace and Security Resolutions or recently the push for certain countries to label policy as explicitly feminist, in the creation of Feminist Foreign Policy. The extent to which these policies actually make women's lives better or can be accurately described as feminist has of course been questioned by feminist scholars (Thomson, 2020) and can perhaps be said to be more of a sign that certain countries ascribe to a particular liberal international order rather than having the potential to radically restructure societies or politics in favour of women. The contemporary global neo-liberal political climate has made feminists question the relationship with the state, with arguments that the institutionalisation or co-option of feminism by the state and corporate world serves a particular ideological function under capitalism which aims to marketise and individualise feminism and weakens the radical potential of feminism as a political and collective movement (Fraser, 2016).

The prefigurative politics and strategies in abortion movements and the relationship of abortion to the state is an ongoing discussion which has been particularly prevalent in the Latin American context. The dissemination of knowledge and information about abortion and abortion access across borders has been accompanied by other developments in autonomous care models such as setting up information hotlines and accompaniment models (similar to the abortion doula model presented below) challenging paternalistic and hierarchical modes of formal healthcare routes to abortion (Assis and Erdman, 2022; Duffy et al., 2023) These models of care have been described as explicitly prefigurative and feminist through their provision of comprehensive care, direct action and horizontal power relations. In some of these groups, relationships with the state and state provision of care are explicitly rejected. Within contemporary abortion politics there is an ongoing conversation between feminist care ethics, abortion care provision and prefigurative strategies of feminist abortion rights groups into which this chapter intervenes.

Theories of care

Feminist care theorists recognize that care is a complex political terrain. This body of work acknowledges that care relations are power relations, who cares, whose care needs matter and how care is valued within society all contain the potential for exploitation, dominance and inequality. The role of the state in care is often found to be one where carelessness abounds and where care can be withheld from certain groups in society. Since the outbreak of the COVID-19 pandemic, care has again become prominent in political discussions and thought and has reinvigorated care ethics debates and the rethinking of care relations and the value society affords care, whether these discussions remain in public consciousness in the long term remains to be seen. More recent accounts of care, specifically those from LGBT+ and disability activists, have understood care as a prefigurative practice, a creative act, one through which alternative futures become possible and are created every day (Sharman, 2023: 13). These hopeful, yet critical, accounts see the transformative possibilities of care work through the everyday and collective practice of care and that its prefigurative potential is through the act of doing. As Joan Tronto has written in the development of a politics of care we must 'start in the middle of things. Care practices don't suddenly begin, they are already ongoing' (Tronto, 2015: 4).

Feminist interventions into care began in the 1980s and have attempted to make care visible as a predominantly private sphere activity and to make it central to our understandings of politics and society. Seminal work on care ethics contributes to our understandings of care and also its wider potential transformative political potential. One of the most well-known pieces of work on care ethics is Sara Ruddick's *Maternal Thinking* (1980) which argued that care work goes beyond women's role in social reproduction and that the thinking that arises from mothering may be used as a 'standpoint from which to criticize the destructiveness of war and begin to reinvent peace' (1980: 12). This work foregrounds the knowledge and experience of carers as one that could radically reform our political ideas and institutions. However, whilst Ruddick does not intend maternal to equal women but to mean any responsible adult who takes care of a child, the use of the term 'maternal' and the explicit link to childcare continues to link women to childcare and centres childcare as the primary or most important form of care work.

Carol Gilligan's *In a Different Voice* (1993), in a rejoinder to an argument in psychology that girls reach a lower level of moral development than boys, argues that psychology has misunderstood girls and women and developed a form of morality which is centred on a male-lens. Gilligan found the girls in her research to favour a relationship-based approach to decision-making, rather than a logic right or wrong approach, indicating that the socialisation of women to take account of others alongside or before themselves is integral to morality. In this work the 'ethic of care' and 'ethic of responsibility' concepts were developed, ethics relating to the responses of other people and to our responsibility for our actions and choices as individuals. Of course, this may go beyond taking others into account, veering into self-sacrificing decisions where one's needs are taken out of the equation. Whilst Gilligan's work has been critiqued it continues to have relevance in bringing gender and care into our understanding of morality and the need for collective consideration in decision-making.

In Joan Tronto's *Moral Boundaries: A Political Argument for an Ethic of Care* (2020) she argues that the association of care with women and with women's morality as well as being inaccurate must be challenged politically to begin moral and political debates about care anew and centre care work within political and social lives. Tronto's work acknowledges the burden of care work is intersectional and falls on working class women and women of colour disproportionately. She introduces a typology of caring based on the categories of caring about, taking care of, care-giving, and care-receiving. In later work on caring democracies, Tronto (2015) argues that people must have more of a voice in the allocation of caring responsibilities and a feedback loop of care giving and receiving (a fifth category – caring with) will enable more trust and solidarity to grow between citizens enabling them to engage in these processes together rather than alone. Again, collectivity and community caring are foregrounded as aspects of good citizenship.

Care also needs to be understood as a form of labour. Social reproduction has been defined as 'the activities and attitudes, behaviours and emotions, responsibilities and relationships directly involved in the maintenance of life on a daily basis and intergenerationally' (Laslett and Brenner, 1989: 382). Social reproduction recognises that care, in the form of care and socialisation of children, care of the elderly, domestic labour, is necessary for the maintenance of existing society and economy and is an often invisibilised, undervalued and highly gendered area of the labour force. As feminist work on social reproduction has focused to a large extent on the private sphere, labour involved in reproducing community relations has been unrecognised and unsupported (Hall, 2020). Social infrastructure, the community spaces and networks where care and social reproduction are often analysed in terms of physical space rather than the gendered form of labour which is involved in maintaining and reproducing these spaces (Hall, 2020; Emejulu and Littler, 2019). These spaces, in the context of cuts to welfare systems, become simultaneously more integral and more difficult to sustain.

Within some feminist thinking on care, the continuance of gendered assumptions about care and the maternal as a model for care have remained unchallenged. Queer and disability theory and praxis provide some interventions which may begin to destabilise gendered assumptions of who undertakes care labour. The radical egalitarian idea of 'promiscuous care' is particularly interesting in this regard. Based on ethics of AIDs activism in the United States during the 1980s, Crimp (1987) highlights the lack of care by the state in response to the virus, apart from stigmatising gay men and promoting abstinence. Promiscuous is used not in the sense of indifference but in the sense of experimenting with ways of being intimate and caring for each other and creating safer sex practices within the community in response to a lack of care by the state and in many cases from families (Crimp, 1987). Crimp concludes that care practices must originate in the affected communities from their own values. Promiscuous can therefore mean 'indiscriminate' that anyone can care for, about, or with anyone. This of course can be applied to the state, the community, the family and the individual. Promiscuous care therefore destabilises our notions of who cares, for whom and why and moves away from care models based on family obligations, towards wider community responsibility.

This promiscuous vision of care can be seen in more recent care visions, often a response to this crisis of care and removal of funding and support by the state. Viewing care as a collective and community-based act brings a 'messy dependency' (Nishida, 2022), where we have responsibility for each other and ourselves not in a sense of obligation or as a chore but as an act of community. This is not to say that these care networks are a utopia and they suffer from levels of overwork and burnout. Community based visions of care offer both theoretical and practical contributions to our understanding of care. They do not mean that the state can remove its responsibility to provide care but should be based on a justice based vision of care being valued in terms of training and pay, the development of care cooperatives and care banks so that care does not depend on access to a partner or traditional family structure but is accessible to all, importantly as Piepzna-Samarasinha says in the context of disability activism, care should not depend on being liked or loved (Piepzna-Samarasinha, 2018).

The current state of care is characterised to be one of crisis. Emma Dowling describes this as a reduction in resources provided to meet a growing need for care (2022). Global policies of austerity have contributed to a hollowing out of welfare states and the reliance for care on extended family networks or private providers. Feminist work has mapped the changes in spaces of care both in terms of its expansion into new spaces (cafes, museums, arts spaces) and also the difficulty of maintaining spaces of community care within the context of austerity (Power and Mee, 2020; Dowling, 2022). In some ways this has pushed care back into the private (and invisibilised) sphere with more care taking places at home. Bowlby and McKie (2019) describe this relationship between policies, services and infrastructure related to care as carescapes. Mapping the carescape within which an individual is located can help to pinpoint areas of concern in access to resources and services.

In terms of how our current carescape is ideologically constituted, Nancy Fraser's work on neoliberalism and feminism views the current financialised form of capitalism to be one which has depleted our capacity for care where the 'male breadwinner' model has now been reconceptualised to be the 'universal breadwinner' where both parents are compelled to overwork. She suggests a 'universal caregiver' model where both parental care and equal opportunities in the workplace are valued (Fraser, 2016). This idea is restated in the recent Care Manifesto (Chatzidakis et al., 2020) which promotes the idea of 'universal care' where care is prioritised and centralised in social, institutional and political arenas. These models require a substantial rethinking, reshaping and revaluing of social reproduction within society and by the state.

Care policy and politics in Northern Ireland

Understanding the carescape in the Northern Ireland context involves an interrogation of both the domestic policy context and the wider context of the UK's programme of austerity, prevalent for the past fifteen years. The programme of austerity and welfare reform rolled out in the UK has been shown to have a substantial impact on women with estimates suggesting that 86 per cent of the savings to the Treasury through tax and benefit changes since 2010 will have come from women (Keen and Cracknell, 2017). A 2013 report by Oxfam shows that women in Northern Ireland are disproportionately affected by austerity, with female unemployment rising to a twenty-five-year high and female earnings as a proportion of male earnings falling.[1] Social support for single parents, those in domestic abuse situations, migrant and disabled women is particularly weak. The British Pregnancy Advisory Service (BPAS) has reported that decision-making around abortion is being impacted by austerity measures and poverty resulting in higher rates of abortion in England and Wales, up by 17 per cent in the years 2022–2023. Women and pregnant people from Northern Ireland have travelled and continue to travel to England for abortion and are counted in these figures.[2] A choice made about abortion in the context of actual or potential poverty removes much of the autonomy from decision-making and a state which also refuses to provide abortion services is removing all choice entirely.

Another aspect of austerity which affects ability to access support for care is the government's introduction of a two-child limit into Housing Benefit, Child Tax Credit and Universal Credit in the summer 2015 budget. This means that a third child born to a household after April 2017 have not been eligible for increases to Child Tax Credit or Universal Credit unless this child has a disability or if another 'exception' applies. This has a disproportionate effect in Northern Ireland where bigger family sizes are common (Women's Regional Consortium, 2023). One of these exceptions is for a child born as a result of 'non-consensual conception'. This has been called the 'rape clause'. It states that a woman can claim for a third or subsequent child if it was conceived 'as a result of a sexual act which you didn't or couldn't consent to' or 'at a time when you were in an abusive relationship, under on-going control or coercion by the other parent of the child'. A woman cannot claim this exemption if she lives with the other parent of the child. However, it states she can qualify whether or not there has been a court case or conviction of a criminal offence. This clause has a particular impact in NI due to Section 5 of the Criminal Law Act (NI) which requires a duty to report the commission of any crime or risk criminalisation themselves. Whilst no victims of rape have ever been prosecuted under this law, there is the potential for it to impact on reporting for tax credit purposes if the offence has never been reported to the police.

The value that the NI Assembly attach to caring is evident in the fact that, at the time of writing, there is no childcare strategy in place in Northern Ireland. A draft ten-year childcare strategy was consulted on in 2015. The Northern Ireland Executive failed to progress it before the collapse of the

Assembly in January 2017 and it remains unpublished. The draft strategy was clear that any resource allocation would be extremely 'constrained' and that financial support to expand childcare places would be 'time limited' with an expectation that providers would aim in the longer term to cover all costs from fees paid by families. It is unlikely that such a model would lead to any long-term progress on childcare in Northern Ireland even if this strategy were to be implemented. In addition to the lack of progress on the childcare strategy, there has been legislative reform in the rest of the UK in recent years with no equivalent in Northern Ireland. The Children and Young People (Scotland) Act 2014, the Childcare Act 2016 in England and the Childcare Funding (Wales) Act 2019 have been accompanied by investment and embedded statutory duties to provide specified numbers of childcare hours for children with some receiving up to thirty free hours per week. Without legislation, investment or an active strategy Northern Ireland is falling further behind. The only free hours that parents can access are 12.5 hours per week of funded preschool education for three-year-olds, which must be taken as 2.5 hour slots each day during term time.

The most recent NI Childcare Costs Survey has revealed that childcare costs account for 34 per cent of average household income, much higher than the UK rate of 26.6 per cent, and the OECD average of 11.8 per cent (Employers for Childcare, 2021). The unaffordability of this essential service is obstructing women's access to the labour market, sustaining the gender pay gap and placing extreme pressure on single parents. Lack of access to affordable childcare remains a key barrier to equality for women in Northern Ireland. One third of women in NI are economically inactive, considerably higher than the UK figure of 25 per cent.[3] The most common reason given for economic inactivity is family and home commitments. In addition, Northern Ireland has around 220,000 unpaid carers. Around 69 per cent of those who receive carers allowance are women, yet this allowance is one of the lowest in the benefit system (Women's Regional Consortium, 2023).

The invisibility of care work or the assumption that it will be undertaken on a voluntary and unpaid basis can be seen in the NI COVID-19 Recovery Plan. Whilst the pandemic highlighted globally how much we rely on unpaid and invisible care labour, the NI COVID-19 recovery plan has sections on work, retail, education, travel, family and community, sport and culture it has no specific section on care beyond healthcare. Whilst there is recognition within these sections that all COVID-19 measures must be made with a view to ensuring the healthcare service is not over-burdened there is no recognition of unpaid care duties, be that the care of children who cannot attend school, or of relatives with COVID-19 or of the elderly or those with disabilities. The only mention of unpaid care is the statement 'provide support for unpaid carers' within a section on job creation and growth. There is also limited mention of gender and gender inequality. The focus of the document is on recovering the economy without consideration of the invisible and unpaid labour which upholds and sustains the economy, but which is unsustainable in its current form.

Abortion care before and after decriminalisation

In accounts of abortion care there has often been a correlation made between care accessed outside the law as being unsafe and legal abortion care as safe. Alongside the risk of prosecution for accessing abortion outside legal frameworks, law and medicine have combined to over-regulate and medicalise abortion. However, there is increasing recognition that more liberal laws and good abortion access often do not match up, factors such as conscientious objection, mandatory counselling and waiting periods, lack of facilities providing abortion and strict gestational limits combine in many circumstances to provide a context where abortion is lawful on paper but inaccessible in practice. In addition to this, laws can change. Legal regressions have been seen most recently in countries such as the United States and Poland and indicate that complete reliance on the state for abortion care may be risky.

The equation of safe abortion care with formal healthcare pathways has largely been broken down with the increased use of medical abortions (misoprostol and mifepristone) at earlier gestations and a broader conceptualisation of the arena of abortion care to include activities such as information provision, counselling and abortion accompaniment. The increased use of telemedicine for abortion during the COVID-19 pandemic in countries such as Britain, France and Ireland, and its continuance post-pandemic, has also challenged the role of the medical profession in early medical abortion. In these ways there has been an increased acceptance of self-managed abortion as a safe and less medicalised way of accessing abortion and a questioning of the role of the state in the provision of abortion even in regimes where abortion has been legalised (Duffy et al., 2023; Berro Pizzarosso and Nandagiri, 2021). Erdman et al. (2018), writes that these independent spaces are specifically set up by feminist groups to challenge ideas of self-managed abortion being unsafe or harmful which is reshaping our understanding of safe abortion.

In Northern Ireland, prior to decriminalisation, access to abortion predominantly took three forms. First, there was the legal provision of abortion within NHS healthcare settings in Northern Ireland, due to the heavy legal restrictions this amounted to approximately forty abortions per year being performed in NHS facilities (Bloomer and Hoggart, 2016). In 2012, Marie

Stopes opened a clinic in Belfast where early medical abortion took place within the law, however, no statistics were released on how many abortions took place. The primary method of abortion for those in Northern Ireland was to travel to England to access care, approximately one thousand women per year took this option (Bloomer and Hoggart, 2016). Prior to 2016, those travelling for abortion had to do so at their own cost. More recently with the introduction of global activist abortion providers including Women on Web and Women Help Women, who provide the medical abortion pill to those in legally restrictive regimes, this became an option, and statistics from one provider Women on Web show that nine thousand women from NI contacted them between 2010 and 2020. However, ordering the abortion pill online came with the very real risk that pills could be seized by customs or that those who ordered them could be prosecuted. Between 2006 and 2015, the PSNI reported that they had made eleven arrests related to abortion.

Within this framework of abortion care, some legal and some not, activists worked to support the provision of care to those seeking abortion. Groups such as the Abortion Support Network based in London and Alliance for Choice Belfast and Derry, worked to provide information on where to access abortion and how to access and take the abortion pill, worked as clinic escorts to Marie Stopes clinic in Belfast to help abortion seekers and their families and friends navigate the anti-abortion protestors who regularly congregated outside, and provided support and reassurance and sometimes accompaniment to those accessing abortion. Activists risked prosecution for some activities, with police raids on activists' homes and places of work in 2017 claiming to be searching for abortion pills. Within traditional understandings of abortion activism, with decriminalisation of the law should come the scaling back of activities and in particular the provision of care as it is handed over to the state, for several reasons this has not been the case.

First, after decriminalisation in 2019 which was primarily an act of the Westminster Parliament, there was a concerted effort to halt the formal commissioning of abortion services in Northern Ireland meaning that healthcare providers had to self-organise to provide services on an ad hoc basis. The lack of political will to provide abortion within the new legal framework meant that even during the pandemic, some people had to travel to England to access abortion and some health trusts were unable to provide any services at all. Whilst provision now is much more coordinated and medical abortion is largely accessible, with ongoing training for the future provision of surgical abortion, there continues to be an important role for activists in the provision of information and clarity on abortion provision. Alliance for Choice Belfast have taken their network of support and co-ordinated an abortion doula training programme in consultation with activists and local and regional abortion providers, providing an infrastructure of care and support to abortion seekers which is described as a complement to professional healthcare pathways and an approach which is collective and person-centred. Those providing support have described it as ranging from 'reassurance before, during and after using abortion medication, information sharing, and accompanying abortion seekers to clinics' (Campbell et al., 2021: 1).

Second, there is a continued appetite for self-managed abortion and a need for education around abortion and wider reproductive and sexual health. This need can be attributed to the ongoing stigma surrounding abortion but also a wish to control abortion experiences outside of formal healthcare settings. In this way there is an ongoing role for activism in terms of providing information and challenging stigma. Prior to legal change Alliance for Choice Belfast developed and ran an educational programme which situated abortion within wider conversations about women's rights and the reproductive lifecycle challenging learned religious perspectives on abortion and situated it within a women's rights framework (Bloomer et al., 2017). An online training resource is now being developed in conjunction with the Open University, allowing this knowledge to have a much broader reach in NI and transnationally. Since decriminalisation Alliance for Choice Derry have developed a workshop on how to use the abortion pill and how to challenge abortion stigma, these workshops are important in the continued demedicalisation of abortion and demystifying the abortion experience but also in terms of normalising abortion in a society which up until recently criminalised it under almost all circumstances and operated (and continues to operate) on very strict understandings of women's role in society and limitations on bodily autonomy.

The continuance of abortion care beyond the state after legal change is not a phenomenon which is peculiar to Northern Ireland, the increase in usage of medical abortions in early gestations, increases in conscientious objection by healthcare providers, dis- and misinformation being provided by anti-abortion groups, unclear legal systems and public health information all point to the ways in which abortion care infrastructures do not need to sit solely within formal healthcare routes and can be transformative to the ways in which we understand and experience abortion. They also point to the ongoing need to remove abortion from the criminal law in other jurisdictions as those providing alternative quality systems of care should not risk prosecution and therefore repression by the state for doing so.

Prefigurative strategies

Interrogating the Northern Ireland experience of abortion care before and after legal change through the lens of prefigurative politics can both connect it to broader activist strategies in the past and present, and to its ability to transform understandings of both safe abortion and communities of care. Using Raekstad and Gradin's (2020: 10) definition of prefigurative politics as the deliberate experimental implementation of desired future social relations and practices in the here and now, I want to turn to activists' descriptions and reflections on the work that they do to assess it within the definition. To do this, I focus on the deliberate nature of the activity, that is that activists intend to introduce frameworks which in some ways supplant the state or formal healthcare, the experimental nature of activities and the implementation of desired future social relations and their potential effects on our ideas of care, community and gender relations.

Deliberate intent

Activist strategies in abortion politics have often been viewed to be primarily about securing legal change. More recently with consistent regressions in laws and the acknowledgement that law and access often don't match up, there has been more focus based on wider strategic goals of ensuring abortion access whether within or outside the state and challenging social and political attitudes towards abortion and abortion stigma (Pierson et al., 2022; Drapeau-Bisson, 2020). Whilst there is a recognition that this is a fight which needs to be fought on all fronts (a blend of instrumental and prefigurative strategies) and that feminist goals and voices need to be integrated into all arenas, there is also an awareness that politics, particularly in the local context where ongoing crisis makes decision-making impossible, may not be part of a longer-term solution in terms of securing abortion access and acceptance of abortion in society:

> I will always think that the system was not fit for purpose so even tinkering around the edges – changing this law or introducing that policy – won't be enough for me.[4]

> Devolution is done. Its over for me now – it's a complete circus.[5]

The movement away from state-focused strategies blends strategic as well as prefigurative politics. Legal change on abortion came from a mix of international intervention and movement at Westminster, with no input from the Northern Ireland Assembly (Pierson, 2022). Since decriminalisation, movement at Stormont has been either to attempt to weaken the law or to stop the commissioning of abortion services. In this environment, it makes more sense to focus on setting up scaffolds to ensure abortion access independent of the legal parameters and to focus on educating and challenging abortion stigma and attitudes in society to prevent appetite for regressions in the law. Scaffolds of care can also be valuable for minoritised communities who may find it difficult to engage with state health systems. This approach fits within global movements of abortion care which are demedicalising and destigmatising abortion through an increased focus on self-managed abortion and safe abortion outside of formal healthcare.

However, the state must still be held to account for abortion care and activists do not claim to be completely supplanting formal healthcare on abortion and have worked alongside healthcare providers to set up systems of care, in this way a lot of the work is a wraparound to a formal healthcare route. This is important as recent research in the British context has indicated that health system constraints including workforce constraints, infrastructure requirements, cost and commissioning practices have seen a shift towards medical abortion over surgical, indicating less choice in terms of abortion method (Footman, 2022) and activist centred care should not be used as another means by the state to shift its care responsibility or to deny choice in abortion care experience. However, the continued provision of care outside of the state presents an opportunity to centre people rather than the state in abortion discussions and to ensure a sense of security in terms of abortion, whilst legal regressions cannot always be prevented (see, for example, the United States and Poland) the continuance of non-state-based care ensures a continuity of knowledge, information and care which cannot be taken away by legal and healthcare regressions.

Experimental

One important aspect of prefigurative politics and strategy is that it is making new attempts at organising in order to create new social relations, therefore, it is likely that this will involve experimentation and different ways of organising, these may not always be successful but can allow for new ways of thinking and organising to come through. Activists who had been involved in movement building since the 1970s in Northern Ireland noted that attempting to centre care in activism, particularly as a means to enable women's participation in study, work or activism, has always been a part of feminist organising in the region and part of a needs-based rather than strictly ideological approach to activism:

> We established the first women's refuge in Northern Ireland, I was on the committee for that and we negotiated premises from Queens (University) ... there was also at that time a very rudimentary student creche at Queens at that time

(the 1970's) ... it started off in someone's house and then it moved into a very dilapidated building and grew from there.[6]

The reintroduction of what may be described as second-wave modes of feminist organising can also be seen in experiments with community education on abortion and wider aspects of reproductive rights. Setting education about abortion within a wider frame of the reproductive lifecycle and working on a feminist consciousness raising approach rather than a formal educational approach allows for the introduction of personal experience and the linking of the personal to the political and structural in terms of inequality:

> it was really noticeable in the workshops in working-class women's centres, they'd never been in a space before where it was ok to talk about childbirth and miscarriage or contraception and in those spaces you're not really teaching, you're holding a space for people to discuss. Those spaces are needed and when people share their experiences then it's much easier to see that this isn't an individual problem, it's a systemic problem, it's about how things are set up.[7]

Much of the experimentation around abortion care has arisen through a direct need. As I have written before (Pierson, 2018b) much feminist activism in Northern Ireland has arisen in the identification of the material needs of a community rather than as a strictly ideological approach. The provision of information about abortion, supporting abortion seekers on journeys or with the use of the abortion pill and providing escort services outside clinics – all these came about as direct needs of abortion seekers under a criminalised regime.

With decriminalisation, rather than abandoning these services, they have been codified into programmes that can support the formal healthcare system in the form of abortion doulas (Campbell et al., 2021) and targeted at attempts to normalise abortion within society in the form of abortion stigma workshops (such as those provided by Alliance for Choice Derry). These experimental attempts at new methods of providing care and normalising abortion have been achieved through trial and error and codifying successful techniques into programmes that can and have been translated into other contexts. For example, Alliance for Choice Belfast's Abortion Doula programme has also been delivered to abortion care activists in the Kenyan context.

Implementing future social relations now

As has been demonstrated above, care is not viewed as integral to politics or policy making in Northern Ireland. In fact, policy and provision of care appear to be predicated on a stay-at-home parent model or the reliance on extended family members rather than comprehensive state provision. The invisibility of care can be linked to gendered structures of social reproduction, those who care for children or other relatives are predominantly women and it is viewed to be something that one does out of a duty of love rather than as labour that should be compensated or that contributes to society. Talking about wider notions of care labour within the context of abortion rights was highlighted by activists:

> the job of feminism is to talk about community practices and healing and caring. But all of those things are so feminized and therefore dumbed down.[8]
>
> I think it's linked to reproductive justice and it's about getting this idea of care work away from this like self-sacrificing feminine ideal and actually, realizing it's work.[9]

Abortion care work does not necessarily destabilise our gendered notions of who performs care labour, the majority of activists who undertake this work identify as women. However, it can reorientate our ideas of what care is, as noted in chapter two, much of women's identity in Northern Ireland is focused on the maternal and on a specific ideal of self-sacrificing motherhood. Abortion care focuses on supporting those who do not want to be mothers, or who do not want to be mothers in this particular circumstance, as such it represents a support network that attempts to challenge motherhood as destiny in women's identity construction in Northern Ireland. In addition, this idea of care is promiscuous in that it moves care away from being something that is provided within a nuclear or extended blood family or by individuals, to something that we do communally and collectively, not for those who we love via a sense of duty but for anyone who needs care and support.

One of the fundamental aspects of Northern Ireland politics is its focus on the idea of two communities, that there are two ethno-religious groups in society and all rights and funding must be balanced equally between these two groups in order to maintain some form of stability. This has created a zero-sum game approach whereby if one community is seen to gain something, the other must lose out. Whilst community relations building is an industry in itself, it can be said that this work can also reinforce rather than challenge identity. Feminist activism more broadly can challenge the notion of community and who is viewed to be part of a community, but abortion care outside the state can take this notion further by challenging our ideas of who we should care for and about. Abortion care asks us to be more promiscuous about caring responsibility and to form wider networks of care.

Activists reflected on this expanding notion of care in their own interpretations of their feminism and activism and what they prioritise:

> When I started it was you know – we're gonna smash the patriarchy – and I still very much believe in that. But now I am looking more and more to community care. You know radical acts of love and as I said – how can we reach out to people?[10]

> Alienation ... you know our alienation from each other, not being able to organise collectively had a huge impact during COVID. It's something I worry about, those rituals build community and safety.[11]

The first quote highlights how ideologies can sometimes distance us from caring about each other and care practices whilst the second quote illustrates the increased separation from each other and wider communities that was exacerbated by the pandemic. Feminist modes of care ask us to go beyond simply tolerating or living alongside other groups of people. We are actively being asked to care for and about others outside the traditional limitations of what constitutes our community. This expansive notion of care may do more to challenge material inequalities than either an ideologically pure approach to feminism or the process of advocating for legal change.

Conclusions

The provision of abortion care outside of state healthcare pathways is a feminist act which is a response to both the material need for access and a prefigurative feminist strategy which attempts to move power and governance over abortion away from medical and state authority towards the women and pregnant people who need access to abortion. The activities which comprise abortion care often arise in legally restrictive regimes and are a form of direct action, however, these activities do not need to wither away after legal change, and in fact, in many circumstances are still required. The case of Northern Ireland illustrates how activities developed under a highly restrictive regime continue to develop and expand within decriminalisation.

Whilst these activities aid in abortion access they can also be described as prefigurative. They are a direct experiment in the provision of abortion care beyond the state and fully recognise that the state can take away as well as grant abortion rights. As such, putting information and knowledge into the hands of those seeking abortion, challenging attitudes towards abortion and abortion stigma in society are all part of this strategy which challenges state power to grant or refuse abortions and creates a scaffold of abortion care and knowledge which cannot be dismantled by legal or access regressions.

These activities also have a broader challenge to social relations. Experiments in care will help to shape our understanding and relationship towards care. The neoliberal austerity policies in the wider UK and the lack of care policy and infrastructure in Northern Ireland perpetuate a vision of care which relies on traditional gendered assumptions of who is doing care work and who they are caring for. This closes down the idea of collective community caring and focuses on a nuclear family model. Coupled with Northern Ireland's model of two communities and caring (both literally and politically) for those within our own community, the vision of care is limited. Abortion care models beyond the state have the potential to disrupt our idea of care, this form of care does not tell us who to care for or limit who we can care for. Promiscuity of care labour is a collective endeavour which has the potential to challenge wider social and political relations as well as provide a scaffold to ensure the state cannot rescind or have a monopoly on abortion.

Notes

1 Oxfam. (2013). The true cost of austerity and inequality, Ireland case study. https://www-cdn.oxfam.org/s3fs-public/file_attachments/cs-true-cost-austerity-inequality-ireland-120913-en_0.pdf (last accessed 12/02/2025).
2 https://www.independent.co.uk/news/uk/home-news/abortion-figures-statistics-cause-uk-england-wales-high-austerity-a8678556.html (last accessed 12/02/2025).
3 https://datavis.nisra.gov.uk/economy-and-labour-market/labour_force_survey_annual_summary_report_2023.html (last accessed 12/02/2025).
4 Interview 3, 2022.
5 Interview 9, 2022.
6 Interview 15, 2022.
7 Interview 8, 2022.
8 Interview 8, 2022.
9 Interview 21, 2022.
10 Interview 24, 2022.
11 Interview 21, 2022.

Conclusion

The Northern Ireland peace process has been marketed globally as a success story and blueprint for other societies emerging from violent conflict. Superficial understandings of NI's conflict transformational society have been critiqued and found wanting by scholars in mainstream and critical thought. Similar conclusions could be reached about gender politics in the region. Approximately twenty-five years after the Agreement, both NI's First Minister and Deputy First Minister are women and its archaic abortion laws have been repealed. The success story narrative is seductive; however, it presents only a surface-level understanding of gender politics, ignoring the complex and nuanced ongoing struggles for gendered rights. This is where this text intervenes, attempting to provide a richer understanding and analysis of the role that feminist politics and movement building can play in transforming gender relations and wider political structures and spaces in a post-conflict society.

Taking the approach that critical junctures matter, and that situations of social and political change can also provide space for interventions which disrupt gender relations and inequalities, I argue that the case study of Northern Ireland holds valuable lessons for feminists and gender actors in other regions. It is important to note that I am taking a longer time frame on these critical junctures, and I advocate for other academics studying gender and transitions to take a similar approach. Whilst looking at peace processes and the gendered structure of the institutions and political spaces they set up helps us to see potential inroads for change, taking a longer time frame can illustrate how feminist and gender actors negotiate and potentially shape these spaces over a longer period.

Beyond the context of context of societies in transition, there is the global context of a backlash against feminism and gender rights. Societies which are not considered settled democracies are often left out of feminist narratives which rely on a linear conceptualisation of the progression of rights based on the waves metaphor. Northern Ireland has been considered 'behind' in terms of women's rights; this is most clearly exemplified through the 1967 British Abortion Act not being extended to the region. Within mainstream politics, a history of conflict has also seen NI described as 'a place apart'. However, examinations of feminism in societies which have grown in difficult contexts of violence and the negotiation of different identities can illuminate ways forward for feminism in regressive times.

The feminist movement in NI is an important example of a subaltern counterpublic which has been able to articulate its identities, interests and needs in a context where ethno-national identity has primacy in political debate and policy and law-making. Feminist and gender actors have worked to build a strong collective feminist voice and identity, which negotiates and reflects on difference as a strength, bringing to the fore issues which have been overlooked, ignored or suppressed. This activity has occurred within societal constraints of conservative gender roles and highly masculinised formal political and community spaces. Subaltern counterpublics are seen to emerge via exclusion in dominant debate as a means to create some parity in participation (full parity being impossible unless social inequalities are eliminated). Importantly, as illustrated in this text, these counterpublics do not necessarily have to achieve their goals through dominant political spheres and have broadened our understanding of political space and political activity.

The book addresses the inroads that feminist actors have made in different political spheres in Northern Ireland and the contributions this has made to advancing feminist goals and challenging dominant, conservative ideas of gender identity. It also reflects on ongoing challenges and constraints and the ways in which these can be approached. To conclude the analysis of the text, this chapter summarises the book's main findings and discusses their implications. The book makes the following contributions:

- Conceptually, it contributes to a better understanding of contemporary feminism and feminist organising through a rich examination and analysis of a society often left out of dominant feminist accounts and narratives.
- Empirically, it allows for greater insights into the strategies and discourses used by feminist and gender actors to advocate for political change in different political spaces and the benefits and challenges incurred in movement-building and change-making.
- This is turn helps to illuminate how gender identities shift and change in societies which have undergone substantial transformation and how these shifts relate to broader political changes and advancements in women's rights.

Understanding contemporary feminism

One of the key arguments this book puts forward is that we can advance a much more enriched understanding of contemporary feminism with thicker analysis in a broader range of political and social contexts. Contemporary feminism operates within a global framework where women's and gender rights are both conceptualised as needing advancement by activists, global organisations and states, and at the same time as having gone too far with a need to reinstate more conservative gender norms. In this way, space for feminism is both increasing and shrinking. Within this moment analysing the variety of strategies and discourses of feminist movements is vitally important.

Feminist and gender actors in NI remain grounded in the communities they are advocating for. In this way, feminism operates from a position of pragmatic politics, an awareness of the realities of women's lives and persistent material inequalities. This could be described as a form of feminism which responds to need rather than a particular ideological stance. However, as has been detailed throughout this book there is a reflexive understanding and application of feminist ideas and concepts which form part of this pragmatic politics and in some cases (as with abortion care) the response to material inequality can form part of a prefigurative project which challenges dominant identities and the state as a central actor in women's rights.

Intersectionality is one of the most used terms in contemporary feminist theory and praxis. Considering how the difference between women is recognised and negotiated in feminist movements brings in questions of power and dominance and how movements can be truly inclusive. Feminism in Northern Ireland has been viewed as an ongoing negotiation of identity through work done within communities bridging the dominant ethnonational identities both in the conflict and post-conflict period. NI feminism has also had a distinctly class-orientated approach through the array of women's groups which worked throughout the Troubles to provide spaces for women and service provision in lieu of the state. These negotiations have brought difficult discussions to the fore, for example, neutrality on constitutional issues has often been perceived as being naïve by Republican and Loyalist women.

Such feminism has been analysed through the lens of transversal dialogue, a process of constantly negotiating differences between women through a rooting and shifting approach which recognises difference but does not see it as a barrier to engagement or inclusion. As participants in this study indicated this history of engaging in feminism through an approach which sees difference means that considerations of power and dominance in movements are a question that is considered frequently and considers the term 'woman' as socially constructed in relation to other identities, and in an inclusive and broad sense rather than a narrow biological definition. This is not to say that the goals of intersectional, inclusive feminism are always met but that there is a consistent attempt to renegotiate power relations and to cede power to enable a broader range of voices and bodies in feminist spaces. This reflective approach is vital in both feminist debates (such as the inclusion of trans women or of sex work) and in discussions about the future constitutional status of Northern Ireland which brings ethno-national identity to the fore.

This approach also highlights the importance of intergenerational dialogue. Waves approaches to feminism indicate a separation of ideas and generations. As Kate Manne observes, there is 'an inbuilt or assumed obsolescence for feminist thinking, rather than a model of amendment, addition, and new centers for new discussions' (Manne, 2017: xxi). As I have highlighted throughout the book, groups in NI tend to overlap both in terms of membership and in terms of generation. Cynthia Cockburn emphasises the difference in generations of feminism in Belfast, however, this underestimates the interaction of actors and learnings that take place across groups and activities in a small society. In this way, generations build on each other and share learnings in a horizontal rather than in a top-down approach.

Building a strong collective feminist voice is a means by which to create visions of gender equality and to be able to articulate this in a range of political spaces. One of the strengths of organising in Northern Ireland is size, small geographical space means that there is a strong network of actors who often overlap across both the women's movement and other movements. This collective voice means that the sector can respond quickly to ongoing events, examples of this can be seen in the response to trans exclusionary demonstrations or in the creation of a Feminist COVID-19 Recovery plan based on the Hawaii example. As the women's sector is one of the larger community sectors it has created a trusted network who can then invite broader coalitions of actors into policy making spaces. Strong coalitions are important to ensure that rights-based claims do not become divided for political ends and also to achieve goals as strong coalitions have more lobbying power.

Contemporary feminist organising has been described under the umbrella of the fourth wave. Examining feminism through the lens of Northern Irish organising has shown how many aspects embraced by contemporary feminism are also being negotiated and enacted in NI, however, it also highlights the limitations of the waves metaphor which can fail to take account of ongoing and unresolved issues (such as abortion rights, seen to be a second wave concern, yet one which is now a matter of global regression), the importance of intergenerational discussion and sharing of knowledge, and the importance of localised spaces in the articulation of goals and claims making.

Use of political spaces to advance feminist agendas

The spaces that feminist actors should or can use to advance change and gender transformation are contested. As has been outlined throughout this book within different strands or ideologies of feminism whether feminism has potential in state machineries and policy making, or should be a political ideology which works only in grassroots movements is an ongoing question. Throughout this book I have engaged with these debates in a different way, investigating the ways in which feminists utilise differing spaces to facilitate change including the use of national policy making, international frameworks and grassroots activism. In this way, different arenas of change can be evaluated for their efficacy.

In Chapter 3, feminist engagement with policy making in the NI Assembly helps to think through the different ways that feminist actors can articulate demands and where limitations in advancing feminist goals lie. The cohesive movement and voice noted above have made the women's sector trusted voices when it comes to developing policy relating to gender however legitimacy is more contested when it comes to wider politics connected with ethno-national concerns such as security, policing, or cultural politics. In formal political spheres, feminists must articulate their demands in a way that is intelligible to those working in government. As detailed in the chapter, this brings ideology in. Attempting to articulate a vision of feminism which appeals to policy-makers can mean adopting to a liberal framing of rights and equality as this is what makes sense in these spheres. As explained in the chapter, attempting to articulate visions of feminism which benefit all women does not necessarily fit within frameworks of policy and therefore remains unintelligible. This is a common concern for feminism globally, with fears that feminism is being co-opted to advance neo-liberal goals. Broadening visions of feminism beyond the 'lean-in' approach is an ongoing and difficult process which involves discussions on the roots of gender inequality before developing solutions to 'fix' it.

Abortion rights activism can help conceptualise different strategies to challenge inequalities and provide structures beyond the state to reimagine abortion care. Going beyond legalisation as the core goal for abortion rights is a current issue within global politics as it is increasingly recognised that the state cannot be depended on to legislate for abortion, or to provide easily accessible care. In Chapter 5, alternative ways of thinking about the provision of abortion are conceptualised through the lens of prefigurative politics as a means of organising and creating structures we want to see in the future in the present. In this way, providing scaffolds to formal healthcare, which has been necessary through the lack of progress on abortion provision, shows us ways of reimagining care and caregiving. In this way, activism on abortion illustrates how we can create structures which will make it increasingly harder for the state to control abortion access and regress on issues of gender equality. In addition to this, expansive notions of thinking about care can also help us to expand our networks of care and caring, broadening the range of people who are often 'cared about' in formal political spaces.

Challenging the potential success story narrative, there continue to be issues where progress is slow or stalled. As detailed in Chapter 4, since rates of gender-based violence have been recorded in NI they have steadily risen. Whilst improvements have been noted in terms of the response of the police, there continues to be a huge gap in terms of policy development and prosecution rates. One of the reasons why GBV continues to be difficult to tackle is, I argue, the lack of recognition of such violence on a continuum and connections between the past and present. In many ways, GBV is presented as a 'new' issue or a new type of violence, completely differentiated from that of the past and of conflict.

As demonstrated, this is not the case and the connections of such violence to the past and to the construction of militarised masculinities must be taken into account when attempting to tackle this in the present. Without an approach which can see the interlinking of violence and its effect on contemporary access to justice and gender relations, it is likely that effects and lack of access to justice will continue to be felt by those in communities most affected by conflict. I suggest a means to reinvigorate these conversations may come from the WPS Resolutions which have been successfully vernaculized in the NI context with regard to women's participation in peace-building but provide a framework to go beyond participation to consider past and present GBV and its link to women's peace and security. This approach broadens the issue of GBV beyond the Assembly putting the onus on both the British and Irish governments to broach the issue. This may be necessary to challenge the silence on historical GBV and the lack of political will to tackle this topic.

Conclusions on gender transformations and political change

The gender order in NI has been described as conservative, patriarchal and infused with an ethno-national/religious ideology which prioritises women's role as mothers and sacrifice to the private sphere. Much of the feminist literature on Northern Ireland explains how this impacts on and constrains women's roles in society and politics and the ways in which they have brought about gendered change within these constraints. This literature also points to the fact that spaces open for change and for the redefinition of women's roles and identity, spaces such as conflict and peace processes, but that these spaces are temporal and can shut again quickly when societies wish to return to 'normality,' which can be read as returning to a conservative gender order and roles for women. However, twenty-five years on from the Agreement, as mentioned, we have seen increases in women in formal politics and changes to restrictive legislation on abortion and same-sex marriage. This does not mean that gendered power relations have been completely transformed but that feminist actors have made significant inroads into building a cohesive voice and momentum to challenge gender inequality and articulate a way forward for society. There is still some way to go.

Feminist organising and engaging in NI illustrates a commitment to intersectional practices and an understanding of feminism that needs to improve lives tangibly for all women rather than just some. This is an important historical legacy of feminism in the region and as feminist actors engage with the state and formal politics, they continue to exhibit a commitment to challenging material inequalities rather than a slide into a formal liberal equality framework (whilst this may not always be successfully translated into policy, it opens avenues to think about gender equality differently). Another important legacy, witnessed in contemporary organising is a recognition that the state cannot always be a trusted provider or legislator. In a society where the state has been mistrusted by some communities (for good reason) and has had long periods of disfunction, providing means of achieving gender equality beyond the state has a well-developed legacy and expertise which can be drawn when there are blockages in moving issues forward through formal political routes.

What is often less explicitly named is men's roles in this change. One of the most dominant constructions of masculinity in situations of violent conflict is militarised masculinities, as has been described in the NI context as armed patriarchy. Whilst masculinities are not fixed and static, this version of masculinity continues to hold some power in NI and transforming masculinity has not been considered part of peacebuilding. Women's inclusion therefore into institutions and into wider formal and community politics is conceptualised as an issue of participation, and programmes and training have focused on increasing participation, when in fact it may be more useful to frame it as an issue of exclusion. Male power, dominance and masculinities must be part of this conversation of gender transformation and how politics is framed. Feminists are already having conversations about dominance and power, such as those on race outlined in Chapter 2, conversations on power must also extend to how gender roles may shift and change.

Feminist and gender equality actors are reframing and articulating what politics means, and how politics can be done, in Northern Ireland. This approach, whilst acknowledging that legacies of conflict need to be addressed, sees beyond a focus on relations between the dominant two communities or on post-conflict issues, deemed to be what 'real' politics is about. In this way, it opens up space for political actors to focus on issues beyond the sectarian divide, which may have more of a tangible effect on people's day-to-day lives. This text has remained ambivalent about the future constitutional status of Northern Ireland but it is important to note that if women's voices and a feminist perspective remain peripheral or outside these debates and processes it is likely that any change in the status quo will not necessarily bring many gendered benefits. Opening spaces for a plurality of legitimate actors and voices in politics are vital both in the ongoing process of transforming gender relations and in the process of fashioning the future of Northern Ireland.

References

Aggestam, K., Bergman Rosamond, A., and Kronsell, A. (2019). Theorising feminist foreign policy. *International Relations*, 33(1), 23–39.
Ahmed, S. (2007). 'You end up doing the document rather than doing the doing': Diversity, race equality and the politics of documentation. *Ethnic and Racial Studies*, 30(4), 590–609.
Ahmed, Y., Duddy, S., Hackett, C., Lundy, P., McCallan, M., McKeown, G., and Schulz, P. (2016). Developing gender principles for dealing with the legacy of the past. *International Journal of Transitional Justice*, 10(3), 527–537.
Alison, M. (2004). Women as agents of political violence: Gendering security. *Security Dialogue*, 35(4), 447–463.
Alter, K. J., and Zürn, M. (2020). Conceptualising backlash politics: Introduction to a special issue on backlash politics in comparison. *The British Journal of Politics and International Relations*, 22(4), 563–584.
Anderson, M. (2016). *Windows of Opportunity: How Women Seize Peace Negotiations for Political Change*. New York: Oxford University Press.
Andrew, A., Cattan, S., Costa Dias, M., Farquharson, C., Kraftman, L., Krutikova, S., and Sevilla, A. (2022). The gendered division of paid and domestic work under lockdown. *Fiscal Studies*, 43(4), 325–340.
Anthias, F., and Yuval-Davis, N. (1989). *Woman-Nation-State*. New York: Springer.
Aretxaga, B. (1997). *Shattering Silence: Women, Nationalism, and Political Subjectivity in Northern Ireland*. Princeton, NJ: Princeton University Press.
Aroussi, S. (2017). Women, peace, and security and the DRC: Time to rethink wartime sexual violence as gender-based violence? *Politics & Gender*, 13(3), 488–515.
Ashe, F. (2006). The Virgin Mary connection: Reflecting on feminism and Northern Irish politics. *Critical Review of International Social and Political Philosophy*, 9(4), 573–588.
Ashe, F. (2007). Gendering ethno-nationalist conflict in Northern Ireland: A comparative analysis of nationalist women's political protests. *Ethnic and Racial Studies*, 30(5), 766–786.
Ashe, F. (2009). Iris Robinson's excitable speech: Sexuality and conflict transformation in Northern Ireland. *Politics*, 29(1), 20–27.

Ashe, F. (2012). Gendering war and peace: Militarized masculinities in Northern Ireland. *Men and Masculinities*, 15(3), 230–248.

Ashe, F. (2019a). Sexuality and gender identity in transitional societies: Peacebuilding and counterhegemonic politics. *International Journal of Transitional Justice*, 13(3), 435–457.

Ashe F. (2019b). *Gender, Nationalism and Conflict Transformation*. London: Routledge.

Ashe, F. (2024). Gendering constitutional change in Northern Ireland: Participation, processes and power. *Political Studies*, 72(2), 486–504.

Ashe, F., and Harland, K. (2014). Troubling masculinities: Changing patterns of violent masculinities in a society emerging from political conflict. *Studies in Conflict & Terrorism*, 37(9), 747–762.

Assembly and Executive Review Committee. (2015). *Report on Women in Politics and the Northern Ireland Assembly*. http://www.niassembly.gov.uk/globalassets/documents/assembly-and-executive-review-2011---2016/reports/report-on-women-in-politics.pdf (last accessed 17/11/2023).

Assis, M. P., and Erdman, J. N. (2022). Abortion rights beyond the medico-legal paradigm. *Global Public Health*, 17(10), 2235–2250.

Aune, K., and Redfern, C. (2010). *Reclaiming the F Word: The New Feminist Movement*. London: Zed Books.

Bairner, A. (1999). Masculinity, violence and the Irish peace process. *Capital and Class*, 23(3), 125–144.

Beamish, T. D., and Luebbers, A. J. (2009). Alliance building across social movements: Bridging difference in a peace and justice coalition. *Social Problems*, 56(4), 647–676.

Bell, C. (2015). *Unsettling Bargains? Power-sharing and the Inclusion of Women in Peace Negotiations*. Political Settlements Reports, Political Settlements Research Programme. http://www.politicalsettlements.org/files/2015/10/Unsettling-Bargains-8-October-2015.pdf (last accessed 30/09/2024).

Benschop, Y., and Verloo, M. (2006). Sisyphus' sisters: Can gender mainstreaming escape the genderedness of organizations? *Journal of Gender Studies*, 15(1), 19–33.

Berro Pizzarossa, L., and Nandagiri, R. (2021). Self-managed abortion: A constellation of actors, a cacophony of laws? *Sexual and Reproductive Health Matters*, 29(1), 23–30.

Bishop, P., and Davis, G. (2002). Mapping public participation in policy choices. *Australian Journal of Public Policy*, 61(1), 14–29.

Bloomer, F. K., and Hoggart, L. (2016). Abortion policy-challenges and opportunities. NI Assembly Knowledge Exchange Seminar Series. https://www.niassembly.gov.uk/globalassets/documents/raise/knowledge_exchange/briefing_papers/series5/dr-bloomer-and-dr-hoggart-version-2.pdf (last accessed 30/09/2024).

Bloomer, F. K, Mackle, D., MacNamara, N., Pierson, C., and Bloomer, S. (2023). *The Workplace as a Site of Abortion Surveillance*. Gender, Work & Organization.

References

Bloomer, F. K., O'Dowd, K., and Macleod, C. (2017). Breaking the silence on abortion: The role of adult community abortion education in fostering resistance to norms. *Culture, Health & Sexuality*, 19(7), 709–722.

Bloomer, F. K, Pierson, C., and Estrada-Claudio, S. (2018). *Reimagining Global Abortion Politics*. Bristol: Policy Press.

Boggs, C. (1977). Marxism, prefigurative communism, and the problem of workers' control. *Radical America*, 11(6), 99–122.

Bowlby, S., and McKie, L. (2019). Care and caring: An ecological framework. *Area*, 51(3), 532–539.

Braun, V., and Clarke, V. (2006). Using thematic analysis in psychology. *Qualitative Research in Psychology*, 3(2), 77–101.

Braun, V., and Clarke, V. (2021). Can I use TA? Should I use TA? Should I not use TA? Comparing reflexive thematic analysis and other pattern-based qualitative analytic approaches. *Counselling and Psychotherapy Research*, 21(1), 37–47.

Brown, A., Donaghy, T. B., Mackay, F., and Meehan, E. (2002). Women and constitutional change in Scotland and Northern Ireland. *Parliamentary Affairs*, 55(1), 71–84.

Brownmiller, S. (1975). *Against Our Will: Men, Women and Rape*. Minnesota, MN: Fawcett.

Butler, J. (2009). *Frames of War: When is Life Grievable?* London: Verso.

Byrne, J. (2013). *Flags and Protests: Exploring the Views, Perceptions and Experiences of People Directly and Indirectly Affected by the Flag Protests*. Belfast: Intercomm.

Byrne, S., and McCulloch, A. (2012). Gender, representation and power-sharing in post-conflict institutions. *International Peacekeeping*, 19(5), 565–580.

Campbell, E., Connor, N., Heaney, S., and Bloomer, F. (2021). Training abortion doulas in Northern Ireland: Lessons from a COVID-19 context. *BMJ Sexual & Reproductive Health*, 17, 19–27.

Campbell, E., and Roberts, D. (2024). 'Activism is not a one-lane highway': The digital modalities of alliance for choice and abortion decriminalisation. *Irish Political Studies*, Online First, 1–22.

Caprioli, M. (2005). Primed for violence: The role of gender inequality in predicting internal conflict. *International Studies Quarterly*, 49, 101–178.

Caprioli, M., and Boyer, M. A. (2001). Gender, violence, and international crisis. *Journal of Conflict Resolution*, 45(4), 503–518.

Caren, N., Andrews, K. T., and Lu, T. (2020). Contemporary social movements in a hybrid media environment. *Annual Review of Sociology*, 46, 443–465.

Carr, A. (2014). Women together in the darkest days of the 'Troubles'. *Open Democracy*. https://www.opendemocracy.net/en/5050/women-together-in-darkest-days-of-troubles/ (last accessed 17/11/2023).

Celis, K., and Childs, S. (2020). *Feminist Democratic Representation*. Oxford: Oxford University Press.

Chappell, L. (2000). Interacting with the state: Feminist strategies and political opportunities. *International Feminist Journal of Politics*, 2(2), 244–275.

Chappell, L., and Mackay, F. (2021). Feminist critical friends: Dilemmas of feminist engagement with governance and gender reform agendas. *European Journal of Politics and Gender*, 4(3), 321–340.

Chatzidakis, A., Hakim, J., Litter, J., and Rottenberg, C. (2020). *The Care Manifesto: The Politics of Interdependence*. New York: Verso Books.

Cho, S., Crenshaw, K. W., and McCall, L. (2013). Toward a field of intersectionality studies: Theory, applications, and praxis. *Signs: Journal of Women in Culture and Society*, 38(4), 785–810.

Cockburn, C. (1998). *The Space Between Us: Negotiating Gender and National Identities in Conflict*. London: Zed Books.

Cockburn, C. (2001). The gendered dynamics of armed conflict and political violence. In Moser, C. N., and Clark, F. (eds). *Victims, Perpetrators or Actors?: Gender, Armed Conflict and Political Violence* (13–30). London: Palgrave Macmillan.

Cockburn, C. (2007). *From Where We Stand: War, Women's Activism and Feminist Analysis*. London: Zed Books.

Cockburn, C. (2010). Gender relations as causal in militarization and war. *International Feminist Journal of Politics*, 12(2), 139–157.

Cockburn, C. (2013). A movement stalled: Outcomes of women's campaign for equalities and inclusion in the Northern Ireland peace process. *Interface*, 5(1), 151–182.

Cohn, C. (1987). Sex and death in the rational world of defence intellectuals. *Signs*, 12(4), 687–718.

Collective, C. R. (1977). *The Combahee River Collective Statement*. Mexico: Gato Negro Ediciones.

Connell, R. W. (1995). *Masculinities*. Berkeley, CA: University of California Press.

Connolly, C. (1995). Ourselves alone?: Clar na mBan conference report. *Feminist Review*, 50(1), 118–126.

Connolly, L., and O'Toole, T. (2005). *Documenting Irish Feminisms*. Dublin: Woodfield.

Cook, D. (2002). Consultation for a change? Engaging users and communities in the policy process. *Social Policy and Administration*, 36(5), 516–531.

Corcoran, M. (2004). 'We had to be stronger': The political imprisonment of women in Northern Ireland, 1972–1999. In Ryan, L., and Ward, M. (eds). *Irish Women and Nationalism: Soldiers, New Women and Wicked Hags* (113–132). Dublin: Irish Academic Press.

Cortell, A. P., and Davis Jr, J. W. (2000). Understanding the domestic impact of international norms: A research agenda. *International Studies Review*, 2(1), 65–87.

Crangle, J. (2018). 'Left to fend for themselves': Immigration, race relations and the state in twentieth century Northern Ireland. *Immigrants & Minorities*, 36(1), 20–44.

Crimp, D. (1987). How to have promiscuity in an epidemic. *October*, 43, 237–271.

Crossley, A. D. (2017). *Finding Feminism: Millennial Activists and the Unfinished Gender Revolution*. New York: New York University Press.

References

Cupać, J., and Ebetürk, I. (2020). The personal is global political: The antifeminist backlash in the United Nations. *The British Journal of Politics and International Relations*, 22(4), 702–714.

Davies, P. C., Roulston, C., and Afshar, H. (2000). *Gender, Democracy and Inclusion in Northern Ireland*. London: Palgrave.

Davis, A. Y., Dent, G., Meiners, E. R., and Richie, B. E. (2022). *Abolition Feminism Now* (Vol. 2). Chicago, IL: Haymarket Books.

Day, G., and Thompson, A. (2004). *Theorizing Nationalism*. Hampshire: Palgrave Macmillan.

Dean, J. (2009). Who's afraid of third wave feminism? On the uses of the 'third wave' in British feminist politics. *International Feminist Journal of Politics*, 11(3), 334–352.

Dean, J. (2010). The F-word: Cultural politics and third-wave feminism. In Dean, J. (ed.). *Rethinking Contemporary Feminist Politics* (127–162). London: Palgrave Macmillan.

Dean, J. (2012). On the march or on the margins? Affirmations and erasures of feminist activism in the UK. *European Journal of Women's Studies*, 19(3), 315–329.

Deiana, M. A. (2013). Women's citizenship in Northern Ireland after the 1998 Agreement. *Irish Political Studies*, 28(3), 399–412.

Deiana, M. A., Hagen, J. J., and Roberts, D. (2022). Nevertheless, they persisted. Feminist activism and the politics of crisis in Northern Ireland. *Journal of Gender Studies*, 31(5), 654–667.

Deiana, M. A., and Pierson, C. (2015) Addressing Northern Ireland's incomplete peace: young feminists speak out. *Open Democracy 50:50*. https://www.opendemocracy.net/5050/maria-deiana-claire-pierson/addressing-northern-ireland%E2%80%99s-incomplete-peace-young-feminists-speak (last accessed 30/09/2023)

Della Porta, D. (2020). Protests as critical junctures: Some reflections towards a momentous approach to social movements. *Social Movement Studies*, 19(5–6), 556–575.

Dickel, V., and Evolvi, G. (2023). 'Victims of feminism': Exploring networked misogyny and #MeToo in the manosphere. *Feminist Media Studies*, 23(4), 1392–1408.

Dixon, P., and O'Kane, E. (2011). *Northern Ireland since 1969*. Abingdon: Routledge

Dowler, L. (2002). Till death do us part: Masculinity, friendship, and nationalism in Belfast, Northern Ireland. *Environment and Planning D: Society and Space*, 20(1), 53–71.

Dowling, E. (2022). *The Care Crisis: What Caused It and How Can We End It?* London: Verso Books.

Doyle, J. L., and McWilliams, M. (2020). What difference does peace make? Intimate partner violence and violent conflict in Northern Ireland. *Violence against Women*, 26(2), 139–163.

Dragiewicz, M. (2008). Patriarchy reasserted: Fathers' rights and anti-VAWA activism. *Feminist Criminology*, 3(2), 121–144.

Drapeau-Bisson, M. L. (2020). Beyond green and orange: Alliance for Choice – Derry's mobilisation for the decriminalisation of abortion. *Irish Political Studies*, 35(1), 90–114.

Dubnick, M.. and Meehan, E. (2004). *Integrative Governance in Northern Ireland*. Working Paper QU/GOV/16/2004, Belfast: Institute of Governance, Public Policy and Social Research, Queen's University Belfast.

Duffy, D. N., Freeman, C., and Rodríguez Castañeda, S. (2023). Beyond the state: Abortion care activism in Peru. *Signs: Journal of Women in Culture and Society*, 48(3), 609–634.

Edgerton, L. 1986. Public protest, domestic acquiescence: Women in Northern Ireland. In Ridd, R., and Calaway, H. (eds). *Caught Up in Conflict: Women's Responses to Political Strife* (61–79). London: Macmillan.

Edwards, A., and McGrattan, C. (2010). *The Northern Ireland Conflict: A Beginner's Guide*. London: Oneworld Publications.

Eisenstein, H. (1996). *Inside Agitators: Australian Femocrats and the State*. Philadephia, PA: Temple University Press.

Ellerby, K. (2013). (En)gendered security? The complexities of women's inclusion in peace processes. *International Interactions*, 39(4), 435–460.

Elshtain, J. B. (1987). *Women and War*. Chicago, IL: University of Chicago Press.

Emejulu, A., and Littler, J. (2019). We do not have to be vicious, competitive, or managerial. *Soundings*, 73(73), 73–86.

Employers for Childcare (2021). Northern Ireland Childcare Survey 2021. Available online: file:///C:/Users/cpierson/Downloads/northern-ireland-childcare-survey-2021.pdf (last accessed 23/01/2025).

Enloe, C. (1990). *Bananas, Beaches and Bases: Making Feminist Sense of International Politics*. Berkeley, CA: University of California Press.

Enloe, C. (2000). *Maneuvers: The International Politics of Militarizing Women's Lives*. California: University of California Press.

Enloe, C. (2002). Demilitarization – or more of the same? Feminist questions to ask in the postwar moment. In Cockburn, C., and Zarkov, D. (eds). *The Postwar Moment: Militaries, Masculinities and International Peacekeeping* (33–40). London: Lawrence and Wishart.

Equality Commission for Northern Ireland. (2003). *Report on the Implementation of the Section 75 Equality and Good Relations Duties by Public Authorities, 1 January 2000–31 March 2002*. Belfast: Equality Commission NI.

Erdman, J. N., Jelinska, K., and Yanow, S. (2018). Understandings of self-managed abortion as health inequity, harm reduction and social change. *Reproductive Health Matters*, 26(54), 13–19.

Eschle, C., and Maiguashca, B. (2018). Theorising feminist organising in and against neoliberalism: Beyond co-optation and resistance? *European Journal of Politics and Gender*, 1(1–2), 223–239.

Evans, E. (2014). *The Politics of Third Wave Feminisms*. New York: Palgrave Macmillan.

Evans, E. (2016). Intersectionality as feminist praxis in the UK. *Women's Studies International Forum*, 59, 67–75.

Evans, E., and Chamberlain, P. (2015). Critical waves: Exploring feminist identity, discourse and praxis in western feminism. *Social Movement Studies*, 14(4), 396–409.

Fay, M., Morrissey, M., and Smyth, M. (1999). *Northern Ireland's Troubles: The Human Costs*. London: Pluto.

Fearon, K. (1999). *Women's Work: The Story of the Northern Ireland Women's Coalition*. Pennsylvania: Dufour Editions.

Ferree M. M. (2003). Resonance and radicalism: Feminist framing in the abortion debates of the United States and Germany. *American Journal of Sociology*, 109(2), 304–344.

Fitzsimmons, T. (2005). The postconflict postscript: Gender and policing in peace operations. In Mazurana, D., Raven-Roberts, A., and Parpart, J. (eds). *Gender, Security, and Peacekeeping* (185–201). Oxford: Rowman & Littlefield Publishers.

Flesher Fominaya, C. (2010). Collective identity in social movements: Central concepts and debates. *Sociology Compass*, 4(6), 393–404.

Footman, K., Coast, E., Leone, T., Lohr, P., Masters, T., McKay, R., and Glenn-Sansum, C. (2022). Choice within abortion care pathways: Perspectives of abortion care users on abortion methods and service options in England and Wales. LSE E-Prints https://eprints.lse.ac.uk/119219/1/Protocol_4.0_Footman_Choice_in_Abortion_Care_Pathways.pdf (last accessed 30/09/2024).

Fraser, N. (1999). Rethinking the public sphere: A contribution to the critique of actually existing. democracy. In Calhoun, C. (Ed.). *Habermas and the Public Sphere* (109–142). Chicago, IL: MIT Press.

Fraser, N. (2013). *Fortunes of Feminism*. London: Verso.

Fraser, N. (2016). Capitalism's crisis of care. *Dissent*, 63(4), 30–37.

Galligan, Y. (2020). Women MPs from Northern Ireland: Challenges and contributions, 1953–2020. *Open Library of Humanities*, 6(2), 20–32.

Gavrić, S. (2024). Understanding substantive representation of women in consociational post-conflict political systems. *Nationalism and Ethnic Politics*, 30(2), 173–191.

Giles, W. M., and Hyndman, J. (eds). (2004). *Sites of Violence: Gender and Conflict Zones*. Berkeley, CA: University of California Press.

Gillen, J. (2019). Report into the law and procedures in serious sexual offences in Northern Ireland. https://niopa.qub.ac.uk/bitstream/NIOPA/9384/1/gillen-report-may-2019.pdf (last accessed 30/09/2024).

Gilligan, C. (1993). *In a Different Voice: Psychological Theory and Women's Development*. Cambridge, MA: Harvard University Press.

Gilligan, C. (2019). Northern Ireland and the limits of the race relations framework. *Capital & Class*, 43(1), 105–121.

Gilmartin, N. (2018). *Female Combatants After Armed Struggle: Lost in Transition?* London: Routledge.

Gilmartin, N. (2021). Rethinking the post-conflict narrative: Women and the promise of peace in the new Northern Ireland. In Coulter, C., Gilmartin, N., Hayward, K., and Shirlow, P. (eds). *Northern Ireland a Generation After Good Friday:*

Lost Futures and New Horizons in the 'Long Peace' (204–244). Manchester: Manchester University Press.

Gordon, U. (2018). Prefigurative politics between ethical practice and absent promise. *Political Studies*, 66(2), 521–537.

Graeber, D. (2002). The new anarchists. *New Left Review*, 13(6), 61–73.

Graff, A. (2003). Lost between the waves? The paradoxes of feminist chronology and activism in contemporary Poland. *Journal of International Women's Studies*, 4(2), 100–116.

Gray, A. M., and Birrell, D. (2012). Coalition government in Northern Ireland: Social policy and the lowest common denominator thesis. *Social Policy and Society*, 11(1), 15–25.

Gray, A. M., Louise, C., Powell, R., and Harding, S. (2020) *Gender Equality Strategy Expert Advisory Panel Report: Research Thematic Areas, Key Findings and Recommendations*. https://www.communities-ni.gov.uk/system/files/publications/communities/dfc-social-inclusion-strategy-gender-expertadvisory-panel-report.pdf (last accessed 30/09/2024).

Green, J., and Shorrocks, R. (2023). The gender backlash in the vote for Brexit. *Political Behavior*, 45(1), 347–371.

Grosz, E. (2001). *Architecture from the Outside: Essays on Virtual and Real Space*. Chicago, IL: MIT Press.

Hackett, C. (1995). Self-determination: The republican feminist agenda. *Feminist Review*, 50(1), 111–116.

Hagen, J. J. (2016). Queering women, peace and security. *International Affairs*, 92(2), 313–332.

Hagen, J. J., Deiana, M. A., and Roberts, D. (2022). Revisiting gender-neutral policy from a trans perspective: A look at Northern Ireland. *European Journal of Politics and Gender*, 5(1), 145–147.

Hall, S. M. (2020). Social reproduction as social infrastructure. *Soundings*, 76(76), 82–94.

Harkin, C., and Kilmurray, A. (1985). *Working with Women in Derry. Women and Community Work in Northern Ireland*. Belfast: Farset Co-operative Press.

Haughey, S. (2023). *The Northern Ireland Assembly: Reputations and Realities*. London: Taylor & Francis.

Haughey, S., and Loughran, T. (2021). *Bringing the Public Back In: Public Opinion and Power-sharing in Northern Ireland*. University of Liverpool. https://livrepository.liverpool.ac.uk/3146188/1/Bringing-The-Public-Back-In%20%281%29.pdf (last accessed 17/11/2023).

Hauser, G. A. (1998). Civil society and the principle of the public sphere. *Philosophy & Rhetoric*, 31(1), 19–40.

Hayes, B. C., and McAllister, I. (2013). Gender and consociational power-sharing in Northern Ireland. *International Political Science Review*, 34(2), 123–139.

Hayward, K., and McManus, C. (2019). Neither/nor: The rejection of Unionist and Nationalist identities in post-agreement Northern Ireland. *Capital & Class*, 43(1), 139–155.

Hinds, B., and Donnelly, D. (2014). *Women, Peace and Security: Women's Rights and Gender Equality: Strategic Guide and Toolkit.* Belfast: Community Foundation NI.

Hoard, S. (2015). *Gender Expertise in Public Policy.* Basingstoke: Palgrave Macmillan.

Hoewer, M. (2013). UN resolution 1325 in Ireland: Limitations and opportunities of the international framework on women, peace and security. *Irish Political Studies,* 28(3), 450–468.

hooks, b. (2013). *Dig Deep: Beyond Lean in.* The Feminist Wire. https://thefeministwire.com/2013/10/17973/ (last accessed 30/09/2024).

Horgan, G. (2006). Devolution, direct rule and neo-liberal reconstruction in Northern Ireland. *Critical Social Policy,* 26(3), 656–668.

Horn, R., Puffer, E. S., Roesch, E., and Lehmann, H. (2016). 'I don't need an eye for an eye': Women's responses to intimate partner violence in Sierra Leone and Liberia. *Global Public Health,* 11(1–2), 108–121.

Hudson, H. (2005). Doing security as though humans matter: A feminist perspective on gender and the politics of human security. *Security Dialogue,* 36(2), 55–174.

Hunt, S., and Benford, R. (2004). Collective identity, solidarity, and commitment. In Snow, D., Soule, S., and Hanspeter, K. (eds). *The Blackwell Companion to Social Movements* (433–460). Oxford: Blackwell.

Imam, A., and Yuval-Davis, N. (2004). Introduction to warning signs of fundamentalisms. In Imam, A., Morgan, J., and Yuval-Davis, N. (eds). *Women Living Under Muslim Laws* (ix–ixx). Nottingham: The Russell Press.

Ishkanian, A., and Peña Saavedra, A. (2019). The politics and practices of intersectional prefiguration in social movements: The case of Sisters Uncut. *The Sociological Review,* 67(5), 985–1001.

Jankowitz, S. E. (2018). *The Order of Victimhood: Violence, Hierarchy and Building Peace in Northern Ireland.* London: Springer.

Jarman, N. (2008). Security and segregation: Interface barriers in Belfast. *Shared Space,* 6, 21–33.

Jeffrey, C., and Dyson, J. (2021). Geographies of the future: Prefigurative politics. *Progress in Human Geography,* 45(4), 641–658.

Kaplan, E. (2003). Feminist futures: Trauma, the post-9/11 world and a fourth feminism? *Journal of International Women's Studies,* 4(2), 46–59.

Keck, M. E., and Sikkink, K. (1998). *Activists Beyond Borders: Advocacy Networks in International Politics.* Ithaca, NY: Cornell University Press.

Keen, R., and Cracknell, R. (2017). *Estimating the Gender Impact of Tax and Benefits Changes.* London: House of Commons Library.

Keenan-Thomson, T. (2010). *Irish Women and Street Politics, 1956–1973: 'This Could be Contagious'.* Dublin: Irish Academic Press.

Kelly, L. (2000). Wars against women: Sexual violence, sexual politics and the militarised state. In Jacobs, S., Jacobson, R., and Marchbank, J. (eds). *States of Conflict. Gender, Violence and Resistance* (45–65). London: Zed Press.

Kelly, L. (2013). *Surviving Sexual Violence.* Oxford: Blackwell.

Kennedy, R., Pierson, C., and Thomson, J. (2016). Challenging identity hierarchies: Gender and consociational power-sharing. *The British Journal of Politics and International Relations*, 18(3), 618–633.

Killean, R., Dowds, E., and McAlinden, A. M. (eds). (2021). *Sexual Violence on Trial: Local and Comparative Perspectives*. London: Routledge.

Knox, C. (1998). The European model of service delivery: A partnership approach in Northern Ireland. *Public Administration and Development*, 18, 151–168.

Knox, C. (2011). Tackling racism in Northern Ireland: 'The race hate capital of Europe'. *Journal of Social Policy*, 40(2), 387–412.

Kunz, R., and Prügl, E. (2019). Introduction: Gender experts and gender expertise. *European Journal of Politics and Gender*, 2(1), 3–21.

Kwan, J., Sparrow, K., Facer-Irwin, E., Thandi, G., Fear, N. T., and MacManus, D. (2020). Prevalence of intimate partner violence perpetration among military populations: A systematic review and meta-analysis. *Aggression and Violent Behavior*, 53, 1014–1019.

Laslett, B., and Brenner, J. (1989). Gender and social reproduction: Historical perspectives. *Annual Review of Sociology*, 15(1), 381–404.

Levi, M., and Murphy, G. H. (2006). Coalitions of contention: The case of the WTO protests in Seattle. *Political Studies*, 54(4), 651–670.

Lijphart, A. (1977). *Democracy in Plural Societies: A Comparative Exploration*. New Haven, CT: Yale University Press.

Lijphart, A. (1991). Constitutional choices for new democracies. *Journal of Democracy*, 2, 72–89.

Lin, C. S., Pykett, A. A., Flanagan, C., and Chávez, K. R. (2016). Engendering the prefigurative: Feminist praxes that bridge a politics of prefigurement and survival. *Journal of Social and Political Psychology*, 4(1), 123–132.

Little, A. (2002). Feminism and the politics of difference in Northern Ireland. *Journal of Political Ideologies*, 7(2), 163–177.

Lombardo, E., Meier, P., and Verloo, M. (eds). (2009). *The Discursive Politics of Gender Equality: Stretching, Bending and Policy-Making*. London: Routledge.

Lovenduski, J. (2005). *State Feminism and Political Representation*. Cambridge: Cambridge University Press.

Lovenduski, J. (2007). Unfinished business: Equality policy and the changing context of state feminism in Great Britain. In Lovenduski, J. (ed.). *Changing State Feminism* (144–163). London: Palgrave Macmillan.

Lowndes, V. (2020). How are political institutions gendered? *Political Studies*, 68(3), 543–564.

Lugones, M. (2003). *Pilgrimages/Peregrinajes: Theorizing Coalition Against Multiple Oppressions*. Lanham, MD: Rowman & Littlefield Publishers.

McAlister, S., Neill, G., Carr, N., and Dwyer, C. (2022). Gender, violence and cultures of silence: Young women and paramilitary violence. *Journal of Youth Studies*, 25(8), 1148–1163.

McCammon, H. J., and Moon, M. (2014). Social movement coalitions. In Della Porta, D., and Diani, M. (eds). *The Oxford Handbook of Social Movements* (326–339). Oxford: Oxford University Press.

McClintock, A. (1993). Family feuds: Gender, nationalism and the family. *Feminist Review*, 44(2), 61–80.

McCulloch, A. (2018). The use and abuse of veto rights in power-sharing systems: Northern Ireland's petition of concern in comparative perspective. *Government and Opposition*, 53(4), 735–756.

McDowell, S. (2008). Commemorating dead 'men': Gendering the past and present in post-conflict Northern Ireland. *Gender, Place and Culture*, 15(4), 335–354.

McEvoy, S. (2009). Loyalist women paramilitaries in Northern Ireland: Beginning a feminist conversation about conflict resolution. *Security Studies*, 18, 262–286.

McGarry, J., and O'Leary, B. (1995). *Explaining Northern Ireland: Broken Images*. Oxford: Blackwell.

Machanda, R. (2001). Ambivalent gains in South Asian conflicts. In Meintjes, S., Turshen, M., and Pillay, A. (eds). *The Aftermath: Women in Post-Conflict Transformation* (3–18). London: Zed Books.

Mackay, F. (2008). The state of women's movement/s in Britain: Ambiguity, complexity and challenges from the periphery. In Grey, S., and Sawer, M. (eds). *Women's Movements* (37–52). London: Routledge.

Mackay, F., Kenny, M., and Chappell, L. (2010). New institutionalism through a gender lens: Towards a feminist institutionalism? *International Political Science Review*, 31(5), 573–588.

Mackay, F., and McAllister, L. (2012). Feminising British politics: Six lessons from devolution in Scotland and Wales. *The Political Quarterly*, 83(4), 730–734.

Mackay, F., and Murtagh, C. (2019). New institutions, new gender rules? A feminist institutionalist lens on women and power sharing. *feminists@law*, 9(1), 1–54.

McKay, S. (1985). Rape and incest in a violent male society. *Fortnight Magazine*, Belfast, May–June 1985, 9–10.

MacKenzie, M., and Foster, A. (2017). Masculinity nostalgia: How war and occupation inspire a yearning for gender order. *Security Dialogue*, 48(3), 206–223.

McLaughlin, E. (2005). Governance and social policy in Northern Ireland (1999–2004): The devolution years and postscript. In *Social Policy Review* 17 (107–124). Bristol: Policy Press.

McLaughlin and Farris (2004) The Section 75 Equality Duty – An Operational Review. NIO. Availiable online: https://orca.cardiff.ac.uk/id/eprint/58386/1/NORTHERN_IRELAND_OFFICE_2004%5E%5E%5E.pdf (last accessed 12/02/2025).

MacNamara, N., Mackle, D., Pierson, C., and Bloomer, F. (2020). Interrogating the politicization of female genital cutting (FGC) within conditions of asymmetrical cultural convergence. A case study of Northern Ireland. *Women's Studies International Forum*, 82(3), 1023–1091.

McWilliams, M. (2002). Women and political activism in Northern Ireland. In Bourke, A. (ed.). *Field Day Anthology of Irish Writing Vol. V: Irish Women's Writing and Traditions* (375–401). Cork: Cork University Press.

McWilliams, M., and Ni Aolain, F. D. (2013). 'There is a war going on you know': Addressing the complexity of violence against women in conflicted and post conflict societies. *Transitional Justice Review*, 1(2), 1–42.

McWilliams, M., and Spence, L. (1996). *Taking Domestic Violence Seriously: Issues for the Criminal and Civil Justice System*. Belfast: HMSO.

Maeckelbergh, M. (2011). Doing is believing: Prefiguration as strategic practice in the alterglobalization movement. *Social Movement Studies*, 10(01), 1–20.

Manne, K. (2017). *Down girl: The logic of misogyny*. Oxford: Oxford University Press.

Martín de la Rosa, V., and Lázaro, L. M. (2019). How women are imagined through conceptual metaphors in United Nations Security Council Resolutions on women, peace and security. *Journal of Gender Studies*, 28(4), 373–386.

Meintjes, S., Turshen, M., and Pillay, A. (2001). *The Aftermath: Women in Post-conflict Transformation*. London: Zed Books.

Melucci, A. (1995). The process of collective identity. In Johnston, H., and Klandermans, B. (eds). *Social Movements and Culture* (41–63). Minneapolis, MN: University of Minnesota Press.

Mitchell, C. (2006). *Religion, Identity and Politics in Northern Ireland: Boundaries of Belonging and Belief*. Aldershot: Ashgate Publishing.

Montgomery, P., and Bell, V. (1986). *Police Response to Wife Assault: A Northern Ireland Study*. Belfast: Northern Ireland Women's Aid Federation.

Moran, J. (2010). Evaluating special branch and the use of informant intelligence in Northern Ireland. *Intelligence and National Security*, 25(1), 1–23.

Moser, C. O. (2001). The gendered continuum of violence and conflict: An operational framework. In Moser, C. N., and Clark, F. (eds). *Victims, Perpetrators or Actors?: Gender, Armed Conflict and Political Violence* (30–53). London: Palgrave Macmillan.

Munro, E. (2013). Feminism: A fourth wave? *Political Insight*, 4(2), 22–25.

Murray, M., Fagan, G. H., and McCusker, P. (2009). Measuring horizontal governance: A review of public consultation by the Northern Ireland government between 2000 and 2004. *Policy & Politics*, 37(4), 553–571.

Murtagh, C. (2008). A transient transition: The cultural and institutional obstacles impeding the Northern Ireland Women's Coalition (NIWC) in its progression from informal to formal politics. *Journal of International Women''s Studies*, 9(2), 41–58.

Nagel, J. (1999). Ethnic troubles: Gender, sexuality and construction of national identity. In Kriesi, H. (ed.). *Nation and National Identity: The European Experience in Perspective* (85–107). West Lafayette, IN: Purdue University Press.

Ní Aoláin, F. (2000). *The Politics of Force: Conflict Management and State Violence in Northern Ireland*. Belfast: Blackstaff Press.

Ní Aoláin, F. (2006). Political violence and gender during times of transition. *Columbia Journal of Gender and Law*, 15(3), 829–849.

Ní Aoláin, F. (2018). The feminist institutional dimensions of power-sharing and political settlements. *Nationalism and Ethnic Politics*, 24(1), 116–132.

Ní Aoláin, F., Haynes, D. F., and Cahn, N. (2011). *On the Frontlines: Gender, War, and the Post-Conflict Process*. Oxford: Oxford University Press.

Nicholas, L. (2024). Young masculinities, masculinism, backlash, and the complexities of fostering change. *Journal of Applied Youth Studies*, 7(1), 1–8.

References

Nikoghosyan, A. (2018). Co-optation of feminism: Gender, militarism and the UNSC Resolution 1325. *Feminist Critique: East European Journal of Feminist and Queer Studies*, 1, 7–15.

Nikolic-Ristanovic, V. (2002). War and the post-war victimisation of women. *European Journal of Crime, Criminal Law and Criminal Justice*, 10, 138–145.

Nishida, A. (2022). *Just Care: Messy Entanglements of Disability, Dependency, and Desire*. Philadelphia, PA: Temple University Press.

O'Brien, M. (2022). Alliance for Choice Derry: Delivering decriminalisation: Activism in the North-West. In Bloomer, F. K., and Campbell, E. (eds). *Decriminalising Abortion in Northern Ireland*, Volume 1: Legislation and Protest (173–184). London: Bloomsbury.

O'Keefe, T. (2012). 'Sometimes it would be nice to be a man': Negotiating gender identities after the Good Friday agreement. In McGrattan, C., and Meehan, E. (eds). *The Politics of Everyday Life* (83–96). Manchester: Manchester University Press.

O'Keefe, T. (2017). Policing unruly women: The state and sexual violence during the Northern Irish troubles. *Women's Studies International Forum*, 62, 69–77.

O'Keefe, T. (2021). Bridge-builder feminism: The feminist movement and conflict in Northern Ireland. *Irish Political Studies*, 36(1), 52–71.

Opsahl, T. (1993). *A Citizens' Inquiry: The Opsahl Report on Northern Ireland*. Dublin: Lilliput Press.

O'Reilly, M., Súilleabháin, A. Ó., and Paffenholz, T. (2015). *Reimagining Peacemaking: Women's Roles in Peace Processes*. https://cve-kenya.org/media/library/Reilly_et_al_2015_Reimagining_Peacemaking_Womens_Roles_in_Peace_Processes.pdf (last accessed 30/09/2024).

O'Rourke, C. (2017). In the matter of an application by Evelyn White for judicial review [2000] NI 432, [2004] NICA 1. In Enright, M., McCandless, J., and O'Donoghue, A. (eds). *Northern/Irish Feminist Judgments: Judges' Troubles and the Gendered Politics of Identity* (250–262). London: Bloomsbury

O'Rourke, C., and Swaine, A. (2017). Gender, violence and reparations in Northern Ireland: A story yet to be told. *The International Journal of Human Rights*, 21(9), 1302–1319.

Otto, D. (2006). A sign of weakness? Disrupting gender certainties in the implementation of Security Council Resolution 1325. *Michigan Journal of Gender and Law*, 13, 113–173.

Pateman, C. (1989). *The Disorder of Women: Democracy, Feminism, and Political Theory*. California: Stanford University Press.

Patten Report. (1999). *A New Beginning: Policing in Northern Ireland. The Independent Commission on Policing in Northern Ireland*. Belfast: Stationary Office.

Pearce, R., Erikainen, S., and Vincent, B. (2020). TERF wars: An introduction. *The Sociological Review*, 68(4), 677–698.

Peretz, T., and Vidmar, C. M. (2021). Men, masculinities, and gender-based violence: The broadening scope of recent research. *Sociology Compass*, 15(3), 128–161.

Phillips, A. (1995). *The Politics of Presence*. Oxford: Oxford University Press.

Phipps, A. (2020). *Me, Not You: The Trouble with Mainstream Feminism*. Manchester: Manchester University Press.

Phipps, A. (2021). White tears, white rage: Victimhood and (as) violence in mainstream feminism. *European Journal of Cultural Studies*, 24(1), 81–93.

Pickering, S. (2001). Engendering resistance: Women and policing in Northern Ireland, *Policing and Society*, 11(3–4), 337–358.

Piepzna-Samarasinha, L. L. (2018). *Care Work: Dreaming Disability Justice*. Vancouver, BC: Arsenal Pulp Press.

Pierson, C. (2015). *Gender Security: Women's Experiences of (in) Security and Policing in Post-Agreement Northern Ireland*. Doctoral dissertation, Ulster University.

Pierson, C. (2018a). Rights versus rites? Catholic women and abortion access in Northern Ireland. In Burgess, T. P. (ed.). *The Contested Identities of Ulster Catholics* (39–55). Cham: Springer.

Pierson, C. (2018b). One step forwards, two steps back: Women's rights 20 years after the Good Friday agreement. *Parliamentary Affairs*, 71(2), 461–481.

Pierson, C. (2019). Gendering peace in Northern Ireland: The role of United Nations Security Council Resolution 1325 on women, peace and security. *Capital & Class*, 43(1), 57–71.

Pierson, C. (2022). Power-sharing and patriarchy: An analysis of the role of the Northern Ireland Assembly in abortion law reform. In Bloomer, F., and Campbell, E. (eds). *Decriminalizing Abortion in Northern Ireland Legislation and Protest* (15–28). London: Bloomsbury Academic Press.

Pierson, C., and Bloomer, F. (2017). Macro- and micro-political vernaculizations of rights: Human rights and abortion discourses in Northern Ireland. *Health and Human Rights Journal*, 19, 173–191.

Pierson, C. and Bloomer, F. (2018). Anti-abortion myths in political discourse. In MacQuarrie, C., Bloomer, F., Pierson, C., and Stettner, S. (eds) *Crossing Troubled Waters: Abortion in Ireland, Northern Ireland, and Prince Edward Island* (184–213). Charlottetown: University of Prince Edward Island Press.

Pierson, C., Bloomer, F., Allamby, L., Campbell, E., Hughes, B., McLaughlin, L., and Powell, R. (2022). After a CEDAW optional protocol inquiry into abortion law: A conversation with activists for change in Northern Ireland. *International Feminist Journal of Politics*, 24(2), 312–328.

Pierson, C., and Radford, K. (2016). *Peacebuilding and the Women's Sector in Northern Ireland*. Belfast: Institute for Conflict Research.

Pierson, C., and Thomson, J. (2018). Allies or opponents? Power-sharing, civil society, and gender. *Nationalism and Ethnic Politics*, 24(1), 100–115.

Pillay, A. (2001). Violence against women in the aftermath. In Meintjes, S., Pillay, A., and Turshen, M. (eds). *The Aftermath: Women in Post-Conflict Transformation* (35–45). London: Palgrave.

Pitkin, H. (1967). *The Concept of Representation*. Los Angeles, CA: University of California Press.

Porter, E. (2000). Risks and responsibilities: Creating dialogical spaces in Northern Ireland. *International Feminist Journal of Politics*, 2(2), 163–184.

References

Potter, M., and MacMillan, A. (2008). *Unionist Women Active in the Conflict in Northern Ireland*. Belfast: Training for Women Network.

Power, E. R., and Mee, K. J. (2020). Housing: An infrastructure of care. *Housing Studies*, 35(3), 484–505.

Pratt, N., and Richter-Devroe, S. (2011). Critically examining UNSCR 1325 on women, peace and security. *International Feminist Journal of Politics*, 13(4), 489–503.

Puechguirbal, N. (2010). Discourses on gender, patriarchy and Resolution 1325: A textual analysis of UN documents. *International Peacekeeping*, 17(2), 172–187.

Puwar, N. (2004). *Space Invaders: Race, Gender and Bodies Out of Place*. Oxford: Berg Publishing.

Racioppi, L., and See, K. O. S. (2000). Ulstermen and loyalist ladies on parade: Gendering unionism in Northern Ireland. *International Feminist Journal of Politics*, 2(1), 1–29.

Raekstad, P., and Gradin, S. S. (2020). *Prefigurative Politics: Building Tomorrow Today*. Bristol: Polity Press.

Robinson, J. (2000). Feminism and the spaces of transformation. *Transactions of the Institute of British Geographers*, 25(3), 285–301.

Roberts, D. (2022). Repeal and Irish partnerships. In Bloomer, F., and Campbell, E. (eds). *Decriminalizing Abortion in Northern Ireland: Allies and Abortion Provision* (17–28). London: Bloomsbury Publishing.

Roberts, S., and Wescott, S. (2024). To quell the problem, we must name the problem: The role of social media 'manfluencers' in boys' sexist behaviours in school settings. *Educational and Developmental Psychologist*, 41(2), 125–128.

Rooney, E., and Swaine, A. (2012). The 'long grass' of agreements: Promise, theory and practice. *International Criminal Law Review*, 12(3), 519–548.

Ross, F. (2019). Professional feminists: Challenging local government inside out. *Gender, Work & Organization*, 26(4), 520–540.

Rottenberg, C. (2014). The rise of neoliberal feminism. *Cultural Studies*, 28(3), 418–437.

Roulston, C. (1989). Women on the margin: The women's movement in Northern Ireland, 1973–1988. *Science & Society*, 53(2), 219–236.

Rouse, M. (2016). In need of a fresh start: Gender equality in post-GFA Northern Ireland. *Northern Ireland Legal Quarterly*, 67, 233.

Rouse, M., Gray, A., Ballantine, J. A., and Turtle, K. (2023). *Gender Audit of the Northern Ireland Programme for Government 2016–21*. (ARK Working Paper Series). https://www.ark.ac.uk/ARK/sites/default/files/2023-03/Gender_Budgeting-3.pdf (last accessed 30/09/2024).

Rowbotham, S. (1985). What do women want? Woman-centred values and the world as it is. *Feminist Review*, 20(1), 49–69.

Rubio-Marín, R. (2006). *What Happened to the Women? Gender and Reparations for Human Rights Violations*. New York: Social Science Research Council.

Ruddick, S. (1980). Maternal thinking. *Feminist Studies*, 6(2), 342–367.

Sales, R. (1997). *Women Divided: Gender, Religion, and Politics in Northern Ireland*. London: Routledge.

Sanquest, C. (2022). London-Irish Abortion Rights Campaign (LIARC). In Bloomer, F., and Campbell, E. (eds). *Decriminalizing Abortion in Northern Ireland: Allies and Abortion Provision* (9–16). London: Bloomsbury Publishing.

Sauer, B., and Wöhl, S. (2011). Feminist perspectives on the internationalization of the state. *Antipode*, 43(1), 108–128.

Saunders, C. (2008). Double-edged swords? Collective identity and solidarity in the environment movement. *British Journal of Sociology*, 59(2), 227–253.

Scaptura, M. N., and Boyle, K. M. (2020). Masculinity threat, 'incel' traits, and violent fantasies among heterosexual men in the United States. *Feminist Criminology*, 15(3), 278–298.

Sharman, Z. (2023). Imagining more care-full futures: Care work as prefigurative praxis. *Essays in Philosophy*, 24(1/2), 11–25.

Shaw, S. (2013). Gender and politics in the devolved assemblies. *Soundings: A Journal of Politics and Culture*, 55(1), 81–93.

Shuman, S. J., Falb, K. L., Cardoso, L. F., Cole, H., Kpebo, D., and Gupta, J. (2016). Perceptions and experiences of intimate partner violence in Abidjan, Côte d'Ivoire. *PLoS One*, 11(6), 101–123.

Smith, G. (2009). *Democratic Innovations: Designing Institutions for Citizen Participation*. Cambridge: Cambridge University Press.

Smyth, M. (2004). The process of demilitarization and the reversibility of the peace process in Northern Ireland. *Terrorism and Political Violence*, 16(3), 544–566.

Srnicek, N., and Williams, A. (2015). *Inventing the Future: Postcapitalism and a World Without Work*. London: Verso Books.

Stall, S., and Stoecker, R. (1998). Community organizing or organizing community? Gender and the crafts of empowerment. *Gender & Society*, 12(6), 729–756.

Stapleton, K., and Wilson, J. (2013). Conflicting categories? Women, conflict and identity in Northern Ireland. *Ethnic and Racial Studies*, 37(11), 2071–2091.

Stone, L. (2014). *Women Transforming Conflict: A Quantitative Analysis of Female Peacemaking*. https://papers.ssrn.com/sol3/papers.cfm?abstract_id=2485242 (last accessed 30/09/2024).

Storer, H. L., and Rodriguez, M. (2020). # Mapping a movement: Social media, feminist hashtags, and movement building in the digital age. *Journal of Community Practice*, 28(2), 160–176.

Swain, D. (2019). Not not but not yet: Present and future in prefigurative politics. *Political Studies*, 67(1), 47–62.

Swaine, A. (2015). Beyond strategic rape and between the public and private: Violence against women in armed conflict. *Human Rights Quarterly*, 37, 755–774.

Swaine, A. (2023). Resurfacing gender: A typology of conflict-related violence against women for the Northern Ireland Troubles. *Violence Against Women*, 29(6–7), 1391–1418.

Sweeney, J. (2014). Anger as topless woman speaks at Stormont. Belfast Telegraph. https://www.belfasttelegraph.co.uk/news/northern-ireland/anger-as-topless-woman-speaks-at-stormont/30078224.html (last accessed 17/11/2023).

Talbot, R. (2004). Female combatants, paramilitary prisoners and the development of feminism in the Republican movement. In Ryan, L., and Ward, M. (eds). *Irish*

Women and Nationalism: Soldiers, New Women and Wicked Hags (132–144). Dublin: Irish Academic Press.

Taylor, V., and Whittier, N. (1992). Collective identity in social movement communities: Lesbian feminist mobilization. In Mueller, C. M., and Morris, A. D. (eds). *Frontiers in Social Movement Theory* (104–129). New Haven, CT: Yale University Press.

Tindall, D. (2023). Social movements and collective action. In Scott, J., and Carrington, P. J. (eds). *The Sage Handbook of Social Network Analysis* (146–161). London: SAGE Publications.

Thomson, J. (2016). Explaining gender equality difference in a devolved system: The case of abortion law in Northern Ireland. *British Politics*, 11, 371–388.

Thomson, J. (2017). Thinking globally, acting locally? The women's sector, international human rights mechanisms and politics in Northern Ireland. *Politics*, 37(1), 82–96.

Thomson, J. (2020). What's feminist about feminist foreign policy? Sweden's and Canada's foreign policy agendas. *International Studies Perspectives*, 21(4), 424–437.

Thomson, J., and Pierson, C. (2018). Can abortion rights be integrated into the women, peace and security agenda? *International Feminist Journal of Politics*, 20(3), 350–365.

Tokar, B. (2003). Review of Joel Kovel, the enemy of nature. *Tikkun*, 18(1), 77–78.

Tonge, J. (2002). *Northern Ireland: Conflict and Change*. London: Pearson.

Tonge, J. (2020). Beyond unionism versus nationalism: The rise of the alliance party of Northern Ireland. *The Political Quarterly*, 91(2), 461–466.

Topping, J., and Byrne, J. (2012). Paramilitary punishments in Belfast: Policing beneath the peace. *Behavioural Sciences of Terrorism and Political Aggression*, 4(1), 41–59.

Törnberg, A. (2021). Prefigurative politics and social change: A typology drawing on transition studies. *Distinktion: Journal of Social Theory*, 22(1), 83–107.

Townsend-Bell, E. (2021). Breaking hegemony: Coalition as decolonial-intersectional praxis. *European Journal of Politics and Gender*, 4(2), 235–253.

Tripp, A. M. (2023). War, revolution, and the expansion of women's political representation. *Politics & Gender*, 19(3), 922–927.

Tronto, J. (2015). Democratic caring and global care responsibilities. In Barnes, M., Brannelly, T., Ward, N. and Ward, N. (eds). *Ethics of Care* (21–30). Bristol: Policy Press.

Tronto, J. (2020). *Moral Boundaries: A Political Argument for an Ethic of Care*. London: Routledge.

True, J., and Wiener, A. (2019). Everyone wants (a) peace: The dynamics of rhetoric and practice on 'women, peace and security'. *International Affairs*, 95(3), 553–574.

Tryggestad, T. L. (2009). Trick or treat? The UN and implementation of security council resolution 1325 on women, peace, and security. *Global Governance: A Review of Multilateralism and International Organizations*, 15(4), 539–557.

Turner, C., and Swaine, A. (2021). *At the Nexus of Participation and Protection: Protection-Related Barriers to Women's Participation in Northern Ireland*. New York: International Peace Institute.

Turtle, K. (2015). Contemporary feminisms in Northern Ireland: Deep roots, fresh shoots. In Fischer, C. and McAuliffe, M. (eds). *Irish Feminisms: Past, Present and Future* (278–301), Dublin: Arlen House.

Uberoi, E., Watson, C., Mutebi, N., Danechi, S., and Bolton, P. (2021). *Women in Politics and Public Life*. House of Commons Library.

Vaughan-Williams, N. (2006). Towards a problematisation of the problematisations that reduce Northern Ireland to a 'problem'. *Critical Review of International Social and Political Philosophy*, 9(4), 513–526.

Vivaldi, L., and Stutzin, V. (2021). Exploring alternative meanings of a feminist and safe abortion in Chile. In Sutton, B. and Vacarezza, N.L. (eds). *Abortion and Democracy* (226–245). London: Routledge.

Ward, R. (2006). *Women, Unionism and Loyalism in Northern Ireland: From 'Tea-makers' to Political Actors*. Dublin: Irish Academy Press.

Wasserfall, R. (1993). Reflexivity, feminism and difference. *Qualitative Sociology*, 16(1), 23–41.

Weldon, S. L., Lusvardi, A., Kelly-Thompson, K., and Forester, S. (2023). Feminist waves, global activism, and gender violence regimes: Genealogy and impact of a global wave. *Women's Studies International Forum*, 99, 1027–1081.

Wilford, R. (1996). Women and politics in Northern Ireland. *Parliamentary Affairs*, 49(1), 41–55.

Wilford, R. (2010). *Aspects of the Belfast Agreement*. Oxford: Oxford University Press.

Whitaker, R. (2008). Gender and the politics of justice in the Northern Ireland peace process: Considering Róisín McAliskey. *Identities: Global Studies in Culture and Power*, 15(1), 1–30.

Wojciechowska, M. (2022). Participation is not enough: An argument for emancipation as a foundation of participatory theorising. *Representation*, 58(2), 155–168.

Women's Regional Consortium. (2023) *Women's Experiences of the Cost-of-Living Crisis in Northern Ireland*. https://www.womensregionalconsortiumni.org.uk/wp-content/uploads/2023/06/Womens-Experiences-of-the-Cost-of-Living-Crisis-in-NI-2.pdf (last accessed 12/02/2025). .

Woodhouse, T., and Ramsbotham, O. (eds). (2000). *Peacekeeping and Conflict Resolution*. London: Routledge.

Wright, H. (2020). 'Masculinities perspectives': Advancing a radical women, peace and security agenda? *International Feminist Journal of Politics*, 22(5), 652–674.

Wulff, S., Bernstein, M., and Taylor, V. (2015). New theoretical directions from the study of gender and sexuality movements: Collective identity, multi-institutional politics, and emotions. In della Porta, D., and Diani, M. (eds). *The Oxford Handbook of Social Movements* (108–132) Oxford: Oxford University Press.

Yates, L. (2021). Prefigurative politics and social movement strategy: The roles of prefiguration in the reproduction, mobilisation and coordination of movements. *Political Studies*, 69(4), 1033–1052.

Young, I. M. (2000). *Inclusion and Democracy*. Oxford: Oxford University Press.

Yuval-Davis, N. (1993). Gender and nation. *Ethnic and Racial Studies*, 16(4), 621–632.

Yuval-Davis, N. (2000). Human/women's rights and feminist transversal politics. In Ferree, M. M., and Tripp, A. M. (eds). *Global Feminism: Transnational Women's Activism, Organizing, and Human Rights* (275–295). New York: New York University Press.

Index

abortion 2, 4, 6, 9, 10, 15, 20, 33, 35, 36, 41, 42, 45, 56, 58, 70, 71, 79, 99, 100, 105–125, 127, 130
   access 20, 36, 45, 106, 111, 117, 118, 120
   activism 15, 20, 45, 58, 105–125, 130
   law 2, 10, 33, 106, 117–121, 126
Alliance for Choice 9, 45, 56, 118, 119
   Belfast 9, 45, 56, 118, 119, 122
   Derry 45, 118, 119, 122
Alliance Party 13, 34, 37, 48
Alternative Ms Ulster 34
Anglo-Irish Agreement 12
Armagh Gaol 24, 27
austerity 10, 46, 74, 110, 114–115

backlash 5, 6, 20, 50, 59, 68, 98–100
Bailey, Clare 34, 36
Belfast City Hall 49
Belfast Feminist Network 9, 46, 47, 57, 58
Bill of Rights for Northern Ireland 70
Brexit 14, 68, 83
British Abortion Act 127
British Pregnancy Advisory Service 115
Butler, Judith 42, 78

Cahill, Máiría 93
Care Manifesto 114
Catholic 11, 13, 19, 24, 26, 36, 48, 49, 69, 93
Civic Forum 6, 12, 29, 62, 66, 73, 74, 81
class 3, 4, 11, 13, 26, 39, 42, 44, 47, 49–52, 68, 79, 80, 83, 110, 112, 122, 128

Cockburn, Cynthia 4, 21, 23, 26, 44, 47, 48, 71, 72, 86, 129
Combahee River Collective 50, 109
Commission on Flags, Identity, Culture and Tradition 30
Communist Party of Ireland 44
consociational 12, 31, 68, 74
   see also power-sharing
Convention for the Elimination of Discrimination against Women (CEDAW) 10, 15, 102
   see also human rights
COVID-19 31, 59, 72, 74, 75, 83, 105, 111, 116, 117, 124, 129
Cumann na mBan 24

Deiana, Maria 3, 9, 31, 46, 47, 59, 72
DemocraShe 77
Democratic Unionist Party (DUP) 13, 14, 22, 29, 34, 35
devolution 15, 31, 32, 120
Domestic Abuse and Civil Proceedings Act 2021 36
Downing Street Declaration 12
Downtown Women's Centre 45

Equality Commission 66
ethno-national 6, 14, 17–22, 24, 27, 30, 31, 33, 37, 42, 44, 48–50, 52, 68, 71, 74, 75, 127
European Convention on Human Rights (ECHR) 12
European Union 31
   see also Brexit

Facebook 46, 57, 58
   see also social media

Index

feminism
  British 2, 4, 51
  fourth wave 3, 14, 41, 42, 46, 47, 50, 56, 129
  Irish 10, 43
  Northern Irish 44
  second wave 41, 129
  third wave 42
feminist foreign policy 67, 110
feminist institutionalism 32
Feminist Review 27
Foster, Arlene 35
Fraser, Nancy 7, 66, 114
Fresh Start Agreement 21, 30, 74

gender
  experts 14, 62–84
  identity 6, 18, 37, 42, 89, 127
  ideology 5, 20, 68
  neutral 70, 71
  order 2, 5, 14, 15, 17–22, 68, 78, 82, 89, 91, 98, 99, 131, 132
  roles 5, 6, 19, 22–24, 28, 33, 35, 44, 85, 88, 90, 98, 101, 127, 133
Gender Equality Strategy 62, 70, 82
Green Party 34, 36

Haass, Richard 30
hate crimes 53
Her Loyal Voice 49
heteronormativity 22
Holy Cross dispute 49
homophobia 22
homophobic 34, 90
human rights 6, 12, 20, 28, 29, 35, 45, 49, 56, 60, 69, 70, 74, 85, 92, 94
  see also Convention for the Elimination of Discrimination against Women

International Women's Day 34, 46
intersectionality 30, 42, 50–54, 60, 128
Irish Abortion Rights Campaign 56
Irish Constitution 56
Irish government 10, 12, 131
Irish language 56
Irish Republican Army (IRA) 11, 19, 24, 93

justice 5, 6, 15, 21, 41, 43–44, 51, 86, 87, 92, 94–98, 101, 103, 108, 114, 123, 131

gender 95
reproductive 108, 123
restorative 21, 95
social 5, 41, 43–44

Let Women Speak 55
LGBT+ 10, 22, 42, 54, 55, 88, 90, 111
Lijphart, Arend 33
Little-Pengelly, Emma 14
Long, Naomi 37
Loyalist 11, 12, 21, 23–25, 28, 49, 50, 93, 96, 128

masculinity 5, 17, 20, 21, 32, 85–104, 132
McAliskey, Bernadette Devlin 27
McWilliams, Monica 44, 92
Meintjes, Sheila 5, 25, 85, 88, 109
MeToo 51, 57
militarisation 20, 89, 98

National Health Service (NHS) 117
Nationalist 11, 13, 19, 22, 23, 47–49, 53, 73, 93, 95, 108
neo-liberal 66, 110, 130
Northern Ireland Abortion Campaign 45
Northern Ireland Act 69, 103
Northern Ireland Assembly 32, 34, 70, 102, 120
Northern Ireland Civil Rights Association 11, 44
Northern Ireland Community Relations Council 9
Northern Ireland Executive 75, 115
  Department for Communities 36, 70
  Department of Education 36
  Department of Health 71, 106
Northern Ireland Forum for Political Dialogue 12, 28
Northern Ireland Human Rights Commission 70
Northern Ireland Office 81, 102
Northern Ireland Women's Coalition (NIWC) 6, 12, 27–29, 71, 73
Northern Ireland Women's Rights Movement 44

Offences Against the Person Act 56
Office of the First Minister and Deputy First Minister 75, 126
O'Hara, Mal 34

O'Keeffe, Theresa 17, 26, 27, 45, 93
O'Neill, Michelle 14, 101
Opsahl Commission 72
O'Sullivan, Meghan 30

Parades Commission 30
paramilitary 11, 12, 20–22, 24, 25, 45, 93–97, 99
patriarchy 3, 20, 98, 124, 132
peace agreement 2, 6, 12, 28–31, 71, 72, 74, 85, 94, 97, 103
peace building 19, 21, 28, 131
Period Products Bill 36
Phipps, Alison 5, 51, 57, 68
Police Service of Northern Ireland (PSNI) 13, 94, 95, 118
policy making 4, 62–84, 87, 103, 122, 129, 130
power-sharing 6, 9, 12, 17, 31–37, 68–69
  see also consociational
Protestant 11, 13, 19, 26, 36, 48, 49, 69
Puwar, Nirmal 6, 67, 76

Queens University 121

race 9, 50, 52, 53, 55, 83, 133
racism 53
rape 46, 58, 85, 88, 92, 93, 95, 101, 115
Reclaim the Agenda 46, 47
Reclaim the Night 46
Republican 11, 12, 21–28, 35, 36, 49, 50, 93, 95, 96, 128
Robinson, Iris 34
Robinson, Peter 29
Royal Ulster Constabulary (RUC) 13, 20

same sex marriage 70
Scotland 32, 95, 116
sectarianism 2, 4, 5, 15, 32, 33, 45, 48, 50, 53, 66, 105, 133
sexism 3, 28, 32, 34
Sex Matters 54
sexuality 3, 4, 10, 19, 22, 31, 34, 83, 88, 101
Sinn Féin 13, 14, 34
Sisters Uncut 51, 110
Social Democratic and Labour Party (SDLP) 13, 29, 36
social media 5, 14, 56–60
  see also Facebook; Twitter
Strategic Framework to End Violence Against Women and Girls 70, 82

trade unions 4, 46, 55
Training for Women Network (TWN) 10, 73
trans 5, 8, 39, 51, 52, 54, 55, 99, 101, 129
  rights 8, 54, 55, 99
  women 5, 39, 51, 52, 55, 101, 129
transphobia 52
transversal dialogue 25–27, 29, 40, 48, 52, 60, 72, 128
Turtle, Kellie 47, 73
Twitter 46
  see also social media

Ulster Defence Association (UDA) 11, 12
Ulster rugby rape trial 46, 58, 59, 101
Ulster Unionist Party (UUP) 13
Ulster Volunteer Force (UVF) 11
Unionist 11–13, 23, 25, 47–49, 53, 73

violence 4–7, 10–12, 15, 18–22, 26, 27, 29, 33, 34, 38, 41, 42, 44–46, 50, 51, 57, 70, 82, 85–104, 131
  domestic 7, 10, 51, 70, 86, 88, 91, 92, 95
  gender based 15, 34, 38, 41, 42, 44, 46, 50, 57, 85–104, 131
  intimate partner 85, 87, 92, 100
  political 4, 11, 18, 26, 33, 94, 97
  sexual 22, 46, 51, 85, 90–92, 94, 102

Wales 32, 95, 115, 116
Westminster 13, 32, 35, 56, 71, 77, 101, 118, 120
women, peace and security 4, 15, 62, 65, 85–104
  National Action Plan 102
  Resolution 9, 15, 85, 89
Women Against Imperialism 27
Women into Politics 45, 77
Women's Aid 46, 70
Women's Liberation Movement 65
Women's News Magazine 9
Women's Platform 10, 73
Women's Policy Group 74
Women's Regional Consortium 74, 115, 116
Women's Resource and Development Agency (WRDA) 10
Women's Support Network (WSN) 10

Young, Iris Marion 67, 75

EU authorised representative for GPSR:
Easy Access System Europe, Mustamäe tee 50,
10621 Tallinn, Estonia
gpsr.requests@easproject.com

www.ingramcontent.com/pod-product-compliance
Lightning Source LLC
LaVergne TN
LVHW011902210625
814311LV00068B/195